GUIDANCE MONOGRAPH SERIES

SHELLEY C. STONE

BRUCE SHERTZER

Editors

GUIDANCE MONOGRAPH SERIES

The general purpose of Houghton Mifflin's Guidance Monograph Series is to provide high quality coverage of topics which are of abiding importance in contemporary counseling and guidance practice. In a rapidly expanding field of endeavor, change and innovation are inevitably present. A trend accompanying such growth is greater and greater specialization. Specialization results in an increased demand for materials which reflect current modifications in guidance practice while simultaneously treating the field in greater depth and detail than commonly found in textbooks and brief journal articles.

The list of eminent contributors to this series assures the reader expert treatment of the areas covered. The monographs are designed for consumers with varying familiarity to the counseling and guidance field. The editors believe that the series will be useful to experienced practitioners as well as beginning students. While these groups may use the monographs with somewhat different goals in mind, both will benefit from the treatment given to content areas.

The content areas treated have been selected because of specific criteria. Among them are timeliness, practicality, and persistency of the issues involved. Above all, the editors have attempted to select topics which are of major substantive concern to counseling and guidance personnel.

Shelley C. Stone

Bruce Shertzer

GESTALT APPROACHES TO COUNSELING

ALLAN DYE
HAROLD HACKNEY
PURDUE UNIVERSITY

HOUGHTON MIFFLIN COMPANY • BOSTON
ATLANTA • DALLAS • GENEVA, ILL. • HOPEWELL, N.J. • PALO ALTO

ISBN: 0–395–200415

Library of Congress Catalog Card
Number: 74–11966

CONTENTS

EDITORS' INTRODUCTION

This monograph focuses upon the background and application of the Gestalt approach to counseling and therapy. While Gestalt psychology and therapy are not new to the field of helping relationships, interest in the Gestalt approach has heightened markedly during the past several years. Precisely why this blend of Freudian and existential thought has edged toward its place in the sun is a question one can only ponder, for undoubtedly many forces contributed. Among these must be found the great interest in and activity of the encounter group movement, the constant quest of those who attempt to provide helping relationships for "new" ways to think and function with those who seek their aid, and the relatively recent emergence of a body of literature on the Gestalt approach.

It should be acknowledged that, fundamentally, the material dealt with in this monograph is an approach to psychotherapy which can be extrapolated, modified, and utilized in the context of counseling. In this regard, Gestalt ideas and methods are no different from those derived from client-centered therapy, behavior therapy, the analytic therapies, etc. That is, virtually any way of operating and conceptualizing the activities called counseling is rooted in one or several theories of therapy which in turn have their taproots deeply embedded in the various theories of personality. For these reasons little is to be gained, and indeed much may be lost, by engaging in the time-honored game of attempting to label this therapy and that counseling. It is the professional's task and responsibility to sort out the appropriate from the inappropriate, the worthwhile from the worthless, the functional idea or activity from the nonfunctional.

Drs. Dye and Hackney write with enthusiasm and interest. Clearly, they see value and utility in Gestalt thought and method as a counseling vehicle. The reader has much to gain from their effort to transmit an understanding of the theory and method of the Gestalt approach.

SHELLEY C. STONE
BRUCE SHERTZER

AUTHORS' INTRODUCTION

The prospect of collaborating in the writing of this monograph has been exciting for us. As counselor educators we have studied and taught Gestalt psychology for several years, and our mutual interests have been vitally re-awakened during the past two years or so by personal experience with this approach to counseling and therapy. Like a good many others engaged in the training and practice of counseling, we lacked sufficient cognitive awareness and understanding of Gestalt philosophy and theory. Our Gestalt gestalt was incomplete, unfinished. Recent experience as members in training workshops and then as counselors employing the Gestalt approach and some of its methodology has enabled a considerable amount of integration.

The concept of the Guidance Monograph Series and the freedom and support proffered by its editors to organize and present material are ideally suited to our wish to tell about this *live-ly,* enabling, and productive approach to counseling. The philosophy and theory of Gestalt psychology and therapy are comprehensively described elsewhere (see Bibliography). Our aim has been to provide a succinct and explicit supplementary reference for counselors and students having an active interest in methodology.

In organizing and writing, however, we were not able to focus immediately on describing and illustrating Gestalt methods and techniques. We thus discovered that the figure-ground explanation of perception was consistent with our experience. Chapter 1 is a brief review of the evolution of counseling approaches with attention to assumptions, goals, and methods. Similarities and differences are noted and the cumulative effects of counseling thought, research, and practice as these are evident in the Gestalt approach are discussed. Chapter 2 describes the origins of Gestalt psychology and traces the people and events that have brought Gestalt therapy into its current prominence. An explication of theoretical assumptions is included since cognitive understanding is a necessary element in achieving closure and, ultimately, control. Finally, Chapter 3 is a description of some commonly used Gestalt procedures, along with comments regarding their appropriate use, brief explanations where necessary, and illustrations. A suggested outline of training experiences is provided and other current books devoted to Gestalt therapy are identified.

We wish to thank Coni Boss for typing the manuscript and especially for enduring our multiple idiosyncrasies. Joe Mowrer is alive and well, and we are grateful for having permission to use his paper on insanity. The editors, Shelley Stone and Bruce Shertzer, are friends and colleagues. We value the encouragement, patience, and trust these two remarkable men have once again demonstrated.

ALLAN DYE
HAROLD HACKNEY

1

Introduction

Some understanding of the past can be useful in responding appropriately in the present. This platitude acquires meaning when the topic is counseling methodologies and the past is separated from the present by a total of less than 100 years. For practical purposes the period is even more brief. The growth and development of counseling into a professional service offered broadly throughout society in schools, universities, hospitals, clinics and community agencies have occurred largely during the past half-century. Thus, the majority of second-generation counselors and psychologists are now somewhere near the middle of their careers, still applying some of their early learnings, eagerly or warily examining current developments, and anticipating new challenges and responses. The current generation of young professionals in counseling is only the third. The number of years that have elapsed from the beginning until now becomes inconsequential when one faces the startling fact that in this field "pioneers" and "space explorers" work side by side, learning from and teaching one another.

We point out that the subject here is approaches to counseling, methods and techniques, rather than philosophy or theories of behavior and personality. The latter have been topics of human concern since the beginning of time. They still are, of course, and since counseling behavior, like all other behaviors, is a manifesting of what one believes or wants or experiences, attention will be given to the basic assumptions from which various methods have accrued.

The period of time being considered begins with the massive contributions of Sigmund Freud and his associates during the late nineteenth century and extends through today. Six relatively distinct stages can be identified during this century or so of development in counseling methodology: The Dark Ages, Analytic Psychology, Trait and Factor Psychology, Phenomenology, Learning and Behaviorism, and Existentialism. Each of the six stages can be characterized by time, assumptions concerning behavior, goals, and methodological approaches to counseling. Our heritage derives cumulatively from all these stages, none of which is actually discrete, for several reasons. We are speaking of people — what they have done, what they have learned, and what they have communicated to one another personally or in writing. There has been a considerable amount of interaction among people representing various assumptions, settings, age groups, and professional concerns. Each stage has been an outgrowth of experience from the stage preceding it. From current and past experience counselors have responded to new challenges that have come with technological, social, political, and economic changes. As a result, two generations of counselors have retained tested, useful thought and practice from the past while finding more effective ways of responding in the present.

Two additional factors which are prominent in our counseling heritage are eclecticism and pragmatism. Stated simply, most counselors and counseling psychologists are practitioners more than theorists; they will use any reasonable and ethical method that may make things better for their clientele. The realities of life in counseling leave little room for rigid adherence to dogma or the blind following of one's early learnings which, relatively speaking, could not have been acquired very long ago. From Freud on, then, the processes of stimulation, trial, discovery, cross-fertilization, and birth of new approaches have been characteristic of the field. A brief review of the six evolutionary stages in counseling methodology follows.

The Dark Ages

Time

The physiological, intellectual, and emotional processes of the human organism have not changed materially during the past 2,000 years or so. In contrast, the nature of the human experience — socially, economically, physically, and philosophically — has been an odyssey of constant change and evolution. The entire history of the human race is, therefore, a description of how the species *homo sapiens* has managed to cope with and survive an unending stream of events, from the discovery of fire to walking in space, from staying alive to finding meaning in life. Each person who lived before, just as we who live now, faced fear, conflict, frustration, and uncertainty. Each person seeks safety; most also seek affection, achievement, and meaning.

Assumptions

In the face of fear or defeat, people turn to one another. Prior to the advent of psychotherapy during the late nineteenth century, people could only seek the counsel of peers, teachers, religious leaders, or other prominent persons. Then, as now, there were many who, by mere virtue of wisdom, caring, sensitivity to people, and their understanding of the human experience, were able to achieve many of the goals sought by contemporary counselors. Included among the outcomes, no doubt, were relief from anxiety, self-acceptance, insight, and new alternatives. But the matter of getting appropriate assistance was undoubtedly a random process. (In view of current training, practice, certification, and delivery of service dilemmas, we wonder if times have really changed!)

The random or perhaps total unavailability of professional counseling assistance for personal concerns seems not to have been a prominent issue in earlier centuries. During the Dark Ages the nature of life was quite different, with daily thought and activity centered upon survival and meeting other basic needs. The dominant ethics were self-sufficiency, regional allegiance or patriotism and, in many instances, strict adherence to and faith in religious beliefs and practice. In brief, life was more physically difficult so that competition for a minimum of resources was intense. The time for facing higher order needs had not come.

One of the characteristics of humans that distinguishes them from other living things is the capacity to think and reason. From the beginning of time, or at least throughout recorded history, the human being has tried to understand him/herself in relation to both his or her behavior and the meaning of existence. We continue to wonder as we write, you as you read. During the Dark Ages, like any other period of time, one could choose from among several popular assumptions in attempting to resolve the various dilemmas of being human: Why do I act as I do? What is the meaning of life? How can I be less troubled, more content? What's going to happen to me? Among the assumptions prevalent during this early period were the predetermined nature of life, conformity, and external locus of control.

The notion that behavior can be changed is relatively modern; that is, our predecessors generally assumed that both the nature of the human being and the behavior patterns of specific individuals were static phenomena. They sought to understand behavior in relation to the will of God, nature's laws, or genetic inheritance. The assumption was that man was the image of God, that the essential processes of both man and society were unchanging so that the purpose of life, if any, was to understand, accept, and conform to the laws of nature. Relatively little was known of earth's physical properties, of human physiology, organizational processes, or any of the forces that are now recognized as having a major influence on human behavior individually and collectively. Good behavior was thus described in terms of conformity, of adhering closely to the role into which one had been born. Role determinants included sex, race, family, region, class, and vocation. In a word, the most important factor in understanding behavior was tradition. Another assumption was that important, basic, permanent differences existed between people in relation to any or all role determinants. Understanding a person's behavior was thus a matter of knowing a great deal about his or her circumstances. Phenomenological and existential philosophies that described reality in terms of individual perceptions were held by a few but did not become popular in the Western world until much later. Rather, it was generally assumed that the individual had very little in the way of power or authority to direct his or her own fate. Life was more a process of responding in order to survive than of initiating in order to create one's destiny.

Strength, or at least durability, was the fundamental personal virtue. The inability to cope in any manner was regarded either as aberrant and accounted for in terms of physical, emotional, or spiritual weakness, or it was regarded as being the will of supernatural forces. Since little or nothing could be done in either event, those who deviated from their roles to a major extent were soon excluded.

Goals

People in the counselor role without training seek first to solve the client's immediate problem, to help fix whatever has gone wrong. The second objective is also a method — to provide answers, to be a source of information and advice. A third goal that is inherent in the former is to "take over" and be responsible for the client in relation to the problem. We can probably assume that pre-twentieth century counselors aspired to having their clients (1) accept the harsh realities, (2) face and resolve them quickly, and (3) get back to normal. Some additional goals are almost always present in such relationships: to be a caring, helpful friend; to accept the basic person who is troubled; and to provide personal support. These goals are most often implicit rather than explicit. Their presence and importance were not discovered until much later, however.

Methods

Primitive societies have been highly similar in their treatment of members who failed to behave appropriately (as expected) as a result of emotional distress. Freedom and responsibility were withdrawn in proportion to the disability. In extreme cases, the individual was driven out, destroyed, or locked in a room. In many instances the same basic procedure is still used. The history of hospitalization and treatment for emotional disorders describes one of the more tragic effects of man's ignorance. Knowledge of the current status of governmental and public support for mental health services provides another stark reminder of the proximity of the past and the progress yet to be made.

Emotional processes remained a mystery, and a dark one at that, until the twentieth century. Psychological functioning, for better or worse, was taken for granted by all but a handful of philosophers and scientists. The majority who lived then could seek help only from family members, friends or leaders.

The available evidence in the form of history, literature, drama, art, and music from earlier cultures suggests that untrained peer counseling hasn't changed much during the past several centuries. Biblical reference to the term "counselor," for example, describes an individual of wisdom, knowledge and judgment serving in the capacity of adviser or teacher. Personal counseling and therapy methods during the Dark Ages included such methods as listening, advising, informing, reassuring, admonishing, and questioning. These and other similar methods are familiar to us; we have all experienced them as both counselor and client in some way throughout our lives. This simple observation holds twofold significance: (1) The human experience is common in important ways that cut across time, civilizations, cultures, and mores, and (2) we in the twentieth century are certain of relatively little more regarding truly effective methods of counseling and therapy than were our earliest ancestors. Stated differently, there is much to be learned about counseling strategies and techniques that might change and improve the quality, perhaps the very nature, of the human experience. Emotional trauma and feelings of emptiness, for example, may not be as unavoidable as we have assumed; joyful, successful living may be less illusory than we've thought.

Analytic Psychology

For many people the term *analytic psychology* is synonymous with the name of Sigmund Freud who is also regarded by many as the founder of psychology in general. These assumptions probably suffer from a fair amount of inaccuracy and a heavy dose of romanticism, but the fact remains that Freud was the first psychologist whose efforts to develop therapeutic treatment methods were widely described. His genius and creativity are amply documented so that his importance to the field of psychology, and to counseling methodology in particular, seems immeasurable.

Time

In describing the analytic psychology stage of development in counseling methodology, therefore, the primary reference is Freud. The period of time in which it developed was approximately 1875 to 1920. Several other psychologists achieved prominence on their own merit during this era; however, the theoretical and methodological influence of Freud was upon them all.

Assumptions

By the late nineteenth century a number of evolutionary cultural events had occurred: the earth's population had increased, tribes had become nations, large cities had been developed, technology and industrialization were gathering momentum, and for a significant number of the earth's inhabitants, particularly in western Europe, the need for survival was no longer constantly prominent. The human race could now devote attention to the quality rather than the mere preservation of life. At the same time, competition for land and power was intense, the pace of life had quickened, and the rate of scientific discovery multiplied at an increasingly rapid rate.

The human race's understanding of its physiological and psychological nature, however, had not kept pace; disease, epidemic and famine were still commonplace, and those forces that torture minds and souls continued to be regarded as incomprehensible, the workings of human-transcending phenomena. In all the world there was a mere handful of physicians and physiologists who suspected that behavior might be a function of something other than genetics, circumstances, and supernatural forces. One of these was Sigmund Freud, a physician, who became curious about the effects of emotions and mental processes upon physical illness. Freud's life, his personal circumstances, and his work are fully documented elsewhere. We think it vital to this discussion of counseling methodology, however, to make some observations about the historical significance of Freud.

By all accounts he was discontented with the traditional practices of physical medicine and aspired to an academic position so that he could engage in psychological research and discovery. Such opportunities were limited in Vienna at that time and were totally inaccessible to a personally and theologically unorthodox Jew. Relegated by these circumstances to private practice he soon began doing alone what he could not be sponsored to do. His interest and practice were soon devoted to the emotional components of such physical symptoms as anxiety, depression, and hysteria. Throughout his career he was influenced in important ways by several people and events. The effects of each experience were incorporated, in turn, into his thinking and theoretical formulations. His understanding of psychological processes contined to emerge until his death in 1939.

The practice of counseling and therapy within the analytic frame of reference is based upon several assumptions that have been described by Bandura (1969), Hall and Lindzey (1970), Patterson (1966), and Ullmann and Krasner (1969). The first is that behavior is an irrational process. Most thoughts, feelings and actions are determined by complex interactions of innate drives, needs, and wants. These processes operate constantly, but they are not experienced consciously nor can they be fully comprehended. In addition, most present behavior is actually determined by past behavior so that experiences during infancy and childhood are of tremendous significance. In reacting to these events patterns are formed that continue to influence behavior throughout life. Another basic assumption is that much of the human experience involves coping with deprivation, frustration, and anxiety, so that in order to survive emotionally, a variety of defense mechanisms is learned.

From the analytic point of view the individual is largely ignorant of both motivating and adapting behaviors. Moment-to-moment behavior is, in effect, a random process in which the person only seems to participate rationally. The actual causes of behavior are deeply imbedded in the past and are obscured by the myriad of daily experiences in which the individual merely manifests symptoms of his/her true nature.

Goals

Successful analysis requires that the client talk. While this may seem mundane as a goal for counseling it cannot be taken for granted. Clients suffering with intensive depression, anxiety, or fear are often unable and/or unwilling to risk even speaking aloud. Since everything depends on their doing so, helping clients become able to speak is a common initial goal. Analytic counseling further requires that the client be able to recall and describe early life experiences, people, objects and events as fully as possible. An additional essential step is the process of counselor and client identification of significant phenomena and patterns of relationships — responses to certain types of people, sequences, emotional reactions, and so on.

During the period of catharsis and recall, both the counselor and the client will hopefully develop useful understandings of the client's dynamics, and it is ordinarily expected that the client will achieve one or more deeply meaningful insights. From these understandings and insights comes a conscious realization of the ways the client gets into trouble. A final goal is to find more satisfying ways of behaving that will possibly resolve or at least minimize the client's problem.

Methods

Freud did more than any other single individual to develop the talking cure. The specific strategies and techniques he used, however, had been employed throughout countless prior centuries by others in the helping role. His methods included, for example, such ordinary activities as speaking, listening, questioning, observation, interpretation, diagnosis, analysis, advice, and instruction. Methodologically, he was innovative in two ways. Although he did not discover and develop hypnosis as an adjunct to therapy, he was among the first to recognize its potential value and incorporate it into his work. He understood the nature of anxiety; consequently, he quickly learned to counter its effects by a number of relaxation techniques such as proceeding slowly, encouraging, and having the client take a comfortable prone position.

The point here is that the actual methods Freud used in his treatment of mental illness consisted of common rather than radical new forms of human behavior. His assumptions about the origins of human behavior, mental illness and therapy were truly revolutionary. Further, these assumptions formed a comprehensive theoretical framework which, in turn, provided focus and direction for conversations with clients. Freud knew what he was looking for, where to look, and what to do with it when he found it.

The advent of Freud's analytic theory of behavior heralded the end of humanity's total ignorance of its inner experience. From this era of enlightenment beginning at about the turn of the century, the search for both healing and meaning has continued and intensified. We note finally that Freud's system of psychoanalysis was the first widely known methodological approach to counseling. Both the theory and its methods continue to be used in virtually every mental health setting and permeate psychological theory of all types.

Trait and Factor Counseling

Time

The trait and factor approach to counseling began to emerge in about 1920 and enjoyed prominence through 1960. Often referred to as "directive" counseling, it was both an outgrowth of several precedents in theoretical and applied psychology and a response to social-cultural events and circumstances of the time.

During the late nineteenth century and the first two decades of the twentieth century the western world had continued the processes of urbanization, industrialization, and governmental reform. The United States had experienced both a civil war and a world war, both of which had created an increasingly larger and more powerful form of federal government. Free public education had at last become a reality and hundreds of public and private colleges and universities were founded across the country. America had become prosperous and powerful. Like an adolescent, its tremendous energies were directed everywhere at once.

The most mobile and productive society in the history of the world was created between 1920 and 1945. These years encompassed growth and expansion, increased population, profit, economic depression, peace, and war. Public governmental systems of education, health, and other life-enhancing services were created. Social reform became a constant process out of which grew the labor movement, welfare and social security systems, to name only a few. Also, emotional distress became part of the American way of life.

Assumptions

By 1920 psychology had emerged as a recognized field of scholarly and professional endeavor. Its heritage consisted of medicine, philosophy, physiology, and the concepts of such founders as Wundt, Charcot, Janet, Breuer, Freud, Jung, Rank, and Adler.

The trait and factor approach to counseling grew from the interaction between psychoanalytic theory and psychological measurement. Freud had established conclusively that mental processes were subject to research and understanding. Almost simultaneously it had been learned that abilities, rates and amounts of learning, and various other traits and factors could be assessed and quantified. Simon and Binet had developed a scale for measuring intelligence, and these measurement principles had been converted to paper and pencil instruments in the form of the Alpha and Beta tests used for military personnel classification during World War I. With relatively rapid and efficient means to measure and quantify particular types of behaviors, and the realization that individuals with additional understanding could change their behavior, the stage was set for a new approach to counseling. And none too soon, we might add, since along with peace, prosperity, and opportunity in a free, industrial society came an increasing demand to make decisions and adapt to a more rapid and complicated way of life.

Trait and factor counseling is predicated upon two basic assumptions. The first is that several behavior-determining personal characteristics can be measured. The second is that a more complete and integrated understanding of abilities, interests, habits, values, and attitudes will enable the client to live more successfully.

Two theoretical orientations were prominent among those who employed the trait and factor approach to counseling. One group contained those grounded in analytic psychology. The new capability of assigning numerical values to the various elements in the analysis of client behavior was regarded as a scientific breakthrough. Another group consisted of counselors who were content to function without a comprehensive theory of personality and behavior. For this group it was sufficient to be able to evaluate specific behavioral traits relevant to the client's concern. By inference, human behavior was regarded as a system of traits and factors, some of genetic origin and some of which were learned. In both cases there was a tendency to think of these phenomena as existing more or less permanently in certain amounts.

Goals

Trait and factor counseling was inherently adaptive; that is, the counselor's goal was to enable the client's maximum use of personal resources within the existing circumstances. The ultimate goal of counseling was successful, wise, and efficient living. In more specific terms the counselor sought to achieve a more complete self-understanding on the part of the client. This was accomplished by means of appraisal, diagnosis, interpretation, and instruction. In many of the educational and occupational settings where trait and factor counseling was used, a common goal of counseling was to facilitate client decision making relative to educational and career planning.

Methods

Counseling based on trait and factor assumptions caught on quickly with many in the helping professions for a number of reasons. For one thing, it appeared to be a scientific procedure just like "real doctors" used. At last, professional humanists could offer a description of their work that lay persons and other professionals alike found comprehensible and logical. Moreover, the trait and factor approach could be learned in a relatively brief period of time and applied in all the new settings in which counseling services were becoming needed — schools, colleges, employment services, and various mental health facilities.

The trait and factor approach is, at least, sequential and systematic, even if it is less than completely scientific. Proponents have formulated the counseling process as occurring in identifiable, though non-mutually exclusive, stages. The number of stages and the description of events in each vary somewhat among authors. It should be understood that the structural sequence of trait and factor counseling is not rigid; that is, each stage can occur more than once, and the order of occurrence is not totally predictable. In a typical, effective counseling experience, however, the initial stage consists primarily of problem identification. Antecedent events and people, nature of the concern, and symptoms are described. This is also a period of catharsis and anxiety reduction. The counselor uses questions, observations, and supportive techniques designed to understand the client and to provide assurance that something can be done.

The second stage consists of conducting an analysis, gathering any and all information that may have relevance. This often calls for one or more types of appraisal such as testing, clinical observations, and examination of educational, medical, or psychological case history material. During this stage the counselor utilizes whatever methods of assessment may be regarded as appropriate.

The information and data are then synthesized and a tentative diagnosis is developed as an attempt is made to understand the client, the circumstances, surrounding elements, sources of conflict, and nature and intensity of the problem. The diagnosis process serves to provide a different and perhaps new perspective for the client. One or more alternate solutions in the form of changed attitude or behavior are suggested. Counselor techniques at this point include informing, interpreting, and suggesting along with the constant use of support and encouragement.

The client has now become increasingly active in his or her own behalf. As a result, for example, the client has become usefully sensitized to thoughts, feelings, and action. In the final stage new learnings and ways of responding are tried and the results are evaluated. These activities continue until counselor and client agree that further counseling is either unnecessary or would be counterproductive. During this final stage the counselor serves largely as a consultant, engaging in such activities as reflection, integration, and suggestion. The central role is reversed as the client assumes increasing amounts of responsibility for deciding, acting, and living with the consequences of decisions and actions.

Phenomenology

In counseling methodology Carl Rogers is to phenomenology as Sigmund Freud is to analytic psychology. Rogers is by far the most widely known author and practitioner of an approach to counseling predicated upon phenomenological assumptions concerning behavior. The following discussion will center upon Rogers' system of client-centered counseling.

Time

During the period beginning in 1940 through approximately 1965, Rogers succeeded in revolutionizing the process of counseling. His first publications appeared in the early 1940s but their impact was undoubtedly diminished temporarily because of World War II. His views and methods departed radically from all other orientations of the time. Naturally, his assumptions and techniques were highly controversial and most early reactions were adverse. By the early 1950s, however, it had become clear that his methods could be proved effective and that another theoretical-methodological breakthrough had been achieved.

In the years immediately following the war, the mood of the nation changed. Peace, freedom, and prosperity became the goals of daily life. Attention and resources were directed to such actualizing activities as education, health, and recreation. Enrollments in schools, colleges, and graduate programs increased rapidly as young people and returning veterans took the path of education as a direct route to personal success and a new, progressive society.

It should be noted that in 1946 there were very few counselor training programs, school guidance was in its infancy, and counseling psychology had only begun to emerge from medically dominated clinical psychology with its emphasis upon diagnosis and evaluation. With the advent of peace came the need to train and educate thousands of counselors, teachers, psychologists, and social workers to assist in the transition from war to peace.

Rogers' application of humanistic philosophy and phenomenological assumptions to the process of counseling coincided closely with the *Zeitgeist* of the 1950s and early 1960s. Client-centered counseling was welcomed as a relatively direct and uncomplicated means by which large numbers of people could be trained in a brief period of time to work effectively with youth and adults experiencing the full range of human concerns. A further attraction was its non-clinical nature. A method had been found whereby virtually any caring person could enter and participate effectively in a helping relationship with another.

An entire generation of post-World War II counselors and psychologists was weaned on client-centered counseling. Prior to 1965, in fact, there were only three widely known styles of counseling (excluding analytic psychotherapy): the trait and factor approach (also referred to as the directive or clinical style), the client-centered approach (also called Rogerian or non-directive style) and the eclectic approach (some idiosyncratic blend of the other two styles). During the two decades following World War II there was continuing debate over the merits of directive vs. non-directive vs. eclectic counseling. The issues were counselor role, appraisal, diagnosis, leading vs. reflecting, and so on.

Assumptions

Those who counsel from the phenomenological orientation hold several assumptions that have been described by Beck (1963) and Shertzer and Stone (1974). The first is that behavior at any moment is determined by the person's phenomenal field, the universe as experienced by the individual at that moment. It is further assumed that present behavior is determined by prior behavior only insofar as the person's phenomenal field is organized at the moment as it was in the past. Phenomenologists observe that the purpose of all behavior is to maintain or enhance the self; most behavior consists of learned actions toward this goal. Client-centered counselors typically do not regard the predicting of behavior as relevant or useful; the ability to do so, however, depends upon an understanding of the client's phenomenal field and how it can change. Finally, behavior change will occur when the phenomenal field or self-concept has been changed or expanded by a fuller understanding by the client of elements in the field such as perceptions, feelings, attitudes, and knowledge of mediating processes.

Goals

The primary goal of client-centered counseling is congruence between experience and awareness. The purpose of counseling is to provide a totally safe, accepting relationship within which the client can experience the freedom to examine thoughts, feelings, values, attitudes, fears, and ways of behaving. A related goal is the appropriate revision of self-concept. Using the freedom provided by the counselor, the individual becomes increasingly able to discover, recognize, and accept troublesome thoughts and feelings which have been experienced but not perceived. Increased feelings of self-acceptance and worth are achieved, and clients of successful client-centered counseling usually describe a heightened sense of freedom and autonomy. A parallel result is the ability to be more fully accepting and tolerant of others.

Methods

The methodology of client-centered counseling represented a sharp departure from previous approaches both in terms of what is and isn't regarded as appropriate counselor behavior. Further, the centrality of the empathic relationship introduced a totally new method-related condition, namely, that effectiveness depends on the counselor's full awareness of his or her own internal processes along with ability to communicate this awareness to the client. This concept, not to mention the means for achieving its goals, was not well understood during the initial years of client-centered counseling's period of prominence. Those who experimented in a mechanistic way with Rogers' "un-counseling" methods were likely to become bewildered and disenchanted.

This sort of reaction was probably more characteristic than atypical, even among those early practitioners who were in theoretical/philosophical harmony with Rogers, for the fact is that the effective use of client-centered counseling requires a great deal of personal and interpersonal awareness on the counselor's part. Some persons apparently acquire a great capacity for empathic understanding as a part of their maturation and socialization experiences. Many others obviously do not, and the mere expression of a preference to engage in counseling professionally contains no assurance that an individual is sufficiently aware of his or her own dynamics to provide the kind of relationship conditions necessary in client-centered counseling. During the 1950s and 1960s relatively little was being done in counselor education and training programs to provide such necessary personal discovery experiences to those in training. It seems likely that Rogers' emphasis upon counselor self-awareness and congruence contributed significantly to the subsequent development and use of sensitivity, encounter, and human relations training in the preparation of counselors, therapists, and others in the helping professions. Moreover, the era of humanism in counseling fostered by the client-centered approach precipitated a number of significant alterations in counselor education and training processes. It became appropriate and perhaps necessary for counselor educators and trainers to engage, some for the first time, in self-exploration and discovery, to relate to students as persons, to learn and demonstrate new counseling methods, to step from behind desks, rostrums and well-worn lecture notes into the vital realities of affective experience.

Those who understood or perhaps merely sensed the viability of client-centered counseling valued its person-to-person nature. No doubt the majority utilized one or more resources for achieving some additional degree of self-awareness and heightened capacity for empathic understanding. Several sources of such gain existed or were created during this era. Some examples are: self-initiated focus on here-and-now affect during counseling, in-service workshops, professional conferences, staff-student encounter ("Process Groups" were a part of some NDEA Guidance and Counseling Institutes during the middle and late 1960s) and sensitivity training programs sponsored by the National Training Laboratories.

The client-centered approach was characterized above as "uncounseling" because history-taking, diagnosis, interpretation, direction, advising, and suggestion were specifically excluded from descriptions of appropriate counselor behavior. Early skeptics concluded that nothing was left since these techniques had become synonymous with counseling and therapy. To be alive and present, while necessary, was hardly sufficient, they asserted!

Client-centered counseling obviously entails more than being a person, however defined. While it is correct to say that fewer "techniques" are employed, it is not true that the approach is simple nor, in our opinion, can it be learned easily. The fact is that client-centered counseling is more a way of experiencing, understanding, and communicating than it is a set of procedures and methods.

Counselors operating within the phenomenological frame of reference seek to provide an open and emotionally safe environment by relating to the client in an accepting, warm, genuine, and empathic manner. Doing so calls for a great deal of listening and attending in an effort to understand what the client is thinking, saying, and feeling. The counselor's full cognitive and affective awareness is upon the client in an attempt to perceive the world in exactly the same ways as the client. We have observed client-centered counselors, for example, who seem able to empathize with another so fully that there appears to have been an identity fusion. This competency is invaluable in client-centered counseling so long as the counselor can also simultaneously maintain a clear sense of his or her own perspectives and identity.

The most widely recognized client-centered counseling technique is reflection of either verbal, affective, or metaphorical messages. In this way the counselor communicates the presence of attending, hearing, accepting, and understanding. Such reflections can be verbatim restatements or paraphrasing. In any event the goal is to reflect as accurately as possible, to serve as a living mirror, so that the client's processes of self-exploration and discovery are facilitated.

Minimal communications such as, "Yes," "Uh-huh," "I understand," and so forth are used to let the client know that the counselor is listening and understanding. Some clients seem to require nothing more. There is also a relatively heavy use of silence during which the client may engage in reflection, being at peace, or preparing for additional disclosure.

The counselor's disclosure of personal here-and-now affective experience is an important part of client-centered methodology. It is also a most difficult technique to use effectively. The intent of counselor self-disclosure is to acknowledge willingness to be known, to underscore the mutuality of being human, to inform the client of his or her impact on another, and to cherish and enhance the client's dignity/integrity by sharing rather than withholding the counselor's own personness in relation to the client.

Learning and Behaviorism

Like the fabled entertainer who becomes an overnight sensation at age fifty after performing thirty years in relative obscurity, learning and behavioral approaches broke into the big-time of counseling after spending more than half a century as stand-ins. The early work of those interested in learning phenomena was directed toward the development of a personality theory, an explanation of human behavior.

Time

Pioneer work with the concepts of stimulus, response, reward and punishment was conducted just after the turn of the century by Pavlov, Watson, Thorndike, and many others. During the subsequent sixty years or so the principles of learning were further identified and refined by countless numbers of studies and experiments with both animals and humans.

Beginning slowly during the mid-1960s and then increasing rapidly during the late 1960s and into the present, various applications of learning theory have been made to counselor training and practice. Just as phenomenology and client-centered counseling were regarded as alien when they entered a semi-scientific and clinical environment in the 1940s, learning theory-oriented counselors were often greeted with disdain and suspicion by a field that was by now dominated by neo-humanists. Those accustomed to hearing, feeling, and empathizing were appalled by such terms as deficiency, contingency, and negative reinforcement. This was an era of new and unstable social dynamics. Federal support for research and training was on the wane, disenfranchised racial minorities and youth were aggressively militant, the war in Vietnam had cast a number of national value conflicts into bold relief, and many forms of the helping professions had come under heavy accountability fire.

Almost suddenly, it seemed, behavior-oriented counselors began reporting that ways had been found to alleviate symptoms, solve some problems completely, and teach new behavior. Behavioral counseling had arrived and continues to emerge as a viable approach not only to counseling but to a wide array of major educational and social concerns as well.

Assumptions

Behavioral counseling rests upon assumptions which have been derived from social learning theories (Bandura, 1969; Bergin and Garfield, 1971; Ullmann and Krasner, 1969). The primary assumption is that all behavior is learned, and both adaptive and maladaptive behaviors are learned according to the same principles, the most important of which are social modeling and operant conditioning. It is further assumed that all behavior, including any that may be regarded as maladaptive, is purposeful whether or not the individual is aware of the purpose. Behavioral counselors largely disregard the effects of early experience, stating rather that behavior is determined by current environmental contingencies. We note here parenthetically that, while client insight about problem origins is not a goal, it is not unusual for this to occur as client and counselor explore various contingencies that impinge upon troublesome behavior.

People who come for counseling almost always want to tell their story, and this process is a part of behavioral counseling. This activity is accepted by behaviorists for its cathartic and releasing effects as opposed to being a source of valuable information concerning whatever problems may now exist. It is assumed that the client's present behavior is determined by past behavior only to the extent that past environmental factors approximate present ones. In behavioral counseling, attention is given to behavioral patterns and sequences so that the predicting of outcomes becomes a necessary competency. Client behavior can be predicted when the counselor understands how all relevant environmental contingencies bear upon the client's life.

A final assumption contains specific implications for the process of counseling from this orientation, namely, that client behavior can be changed as the counselor helps the client either to unlearn maladaptive behaviors or learn new adaptive behaviors. Further, the counselor may assist in arranging environmental contingencies so that new, more desirable responses will be maintained.

Goals

The goal of counseling from a learning theory frame of reference is to learn and consistently engage in more satisfying, appropriate, and less troublesome behavior. In contact with clientele experiencing particular difficulties, this universal goal is stated in the form of behavioral objectives related to desired outcomes. Clients usually begin by describing how badly they feel, what's wrong with their present circumstances, and perhaps some history of how they got into difficulty. An initial goal of behavioral counseling, therefore, is to assist the client in (1) completing the conversation relative to what's currently wrong, and (2) formulating a specific definition of new, more desirable behavior.

We observe here that behavioral counseling is not predicated upon a comprehensive personality theory as are many other approaches. Behaviorists seem to be much less concerned with the nature of man, the purpose of life, and other existential questions.

They adhere primarily to the notion that behavior is learned and proceed on this basis. Consequently, the counseling experience can be directed toward the alleviation of behavioral symptoms either by unlearning (eradication) or by learning a more appropriate response. In other instances there may be no symptomatology other than such feeling reactions as frustration, anger, or despair that accrue from not being able to respond to a given stimulus at all. In the latter case counseling consists of assisting the client in learning one or more ways of behaving in a new or different situation for which the client has not been prepared.

In simple language, people become clients either when something has gone wrong or when the right thing hasn't yet happened. It's certainly possible, furthermore, that both can be true and that the client is unable to differentiate between the two. A final goal of behavioral counseling is to understand the client's problem(s) in order that an effective approach utilizing learning and/or unlearning can be designed and conducted.

Methods

Listening, talking and other traditional forms of communication are basic skills in the behavioral counselor's repertoire of techniques. As a matter of fact, research in behavioral counseling methods and outcomes has established that communication processes are far more significant forms of behavior than had been previously understood. It must suffice here to say that behavioral counselors do not restrict their focus to complex out-of-the-interview behaviors and those strategies that may terminate or adapt them. As with other systematic approaches to counseling, what goes on during the interview is considered highly significant and perhaps characteristic of the client's presenting problem(s).

The following description of behavioral counseling methods corresponds roughly to the order in which they are typically used. Just as learning is a sequential process, so is counseling from the learning theory orientation. It is also true that there are several forms of learning having varying degrees of difficulty and complexity. Some seem almost infinitely intricate, and it is generally agreed that we now understand only the most rudimentary principles and patterns. For this reason a complete cycle of effective counseling will usually consist of one or more replications of one or more parts of the sequence outlined below.

Release, anxiety reduction, and catharsis are initially achieved as the counselor encourages the client to talk and then listens to the client's description of one or more problems. As these are more fully understood, the client is assisted in translating the account to goal statements — definitions of needed or desired outcomes in behavioral terms. This is a crucial process during which the client begins to learn several useful processes: how to discern motives more accurately and to assess their frequency and intensity; how to state wishes in positive, behavioral terms rather than simply feeling bad and dwelling on failures; how to become aware of separate aspects of a dilemma and to order and prioritize them; and finally, how to accept the reality and responsibility of having the ability to choose. More is learned of these phenomena as counseling continues, of course, and these steps in "learning how to learn" can have long-term value as clients respond to new events and circumstances throughout life.

A heavy reliance is placed upon gaining full, accurate information about the problem behavior, the circumstances within which it occurs, other persons and their significance to the client in the problem context, and so on. From this perspective a description or profile of the problem is prepared. Many behavioral counselors then quantify the various elements in the form of frequencies and estimates of intensity. These base-line data then serve as a reference for measuring success as counseling proceeds toward the attainment of stated behavioral goals.

A further step is the identification of existing reinforcers, positive and/or negative, in the client's total life situation. These may or may not be sufficient for accomplishing the desired change; if not, new ones are developed by identifying either rewards or punishment/deprivations whose value is sufficient to interrupt old behavior patterns. With a comprehensive profile of the problem and an understanding of what either reinforces or inhibits the client, a trial learning program is designed and undertaken. The program is modified in whole or part as new information is derived from the client's trial and practice.

Learning is most successful when it is predicated upon success (reward). Some behaviorally-oriented counselors function on this basis exclusively, though negative reinforcement and aversive conditioning have been proved effective for a variety of problem behaviors. There are those for whom any such negative approach creates a personal value conflict and this has become a major professional-ethical issue. Operating on the principle of success requires that learning be a step-by-step, sequential process in which the client demonstrates complete mastery (this can entail multiple successful trials) at each step before proceeding to the next. Progress is noted (perhaps quantified) and recorded at each step throughout the entire sequence. This act in itself serves to reinforce and motivate the client, particularly those who have learned to think, feel, and act only in global terms. Since many dimensions of human experience cannot be accurately described as *totally* anything — successful, complete, satisfying, appropriate — the use of comparisons based upon the client's former and subsequent behavior seems highly appropriate.

Existentialism

The final stage of development in counseling methodology to be described herein emanates from the existential view of the human experience. The most prominent form of an approach to counseling based upon existential assumptions is Gestalt Therapy. Succeeding chapters will explicate Gestalt theory and practice; thus, only enough will be presented here to complete this brief historical review.

Time

In view of the fact that existential thought is the basis for some of the world's oldest cultures, it may seem illogical to select 1970 as the beginning of the existential era of prominence. The focus here, however, is upon specific forms of counseling that have become widely known and utilized in a variety of settings. Only during the past few years have the theory and methodology of Gestalt Therapy been taught, for example, in settings other than the few Gestalt Institutes in this country, two of which were established by Frederick (Fritz) Perls who, with his wife Laura, developed the modern therapy application of Gestalt psychology.

We are again reminded of the relative youth of psychology in general and counseling methodologies in particular by several circumstances. The first is that the most recently evolved counseling approach was developed by a man who was a contemporary and former student of Sigmund Freud, the author of the first well-known approach. During his life Perls saw the creation of therapy as a means of enriching life, witnessed several major evolutions and adaptations on the part of others, pioneered and refined his own view of man, succeeded in developing effective therapeutic applications, and began to understand how our basic social systems could become more suitable to the human organism. Most prominent Gestaltists have worked and learned personally with either Fritz or Laura Perls. A final coincidence is that Gestalt therapy's period of prominence began in approximately 1970, the year in which Fritz Perls died.

Several factors account for the recent popularity of existential thought. In past centuries people valued their mere existence because they had little else. As a means of emotional survival in the face of physical hardships, pain, and imminent death, there was a wish to be in harmony with the universe and one's own nature. There was no basis for aspiration, accumulation or anything other than being aware of existence.

This philosophy has flourished for countless generations in Asia and, to a smaller extent, in Western Europe. Its recent debut in the United States has been successful under different circumstances. Many middle- and upper-class Americans have discovered that having is not being. The great dream of our founders to own everything came true for some, and it was a nightmare of opulence, loneliness, emptiness, nothingness. For the old there are no more wars to win or markets to corner. For the young there is no challenge and even the taste of righteous dissent has become bitter. We have looked everywhere and tried everything in a vain attempt to buy, build, borrow, or steal meaning. Existentialism teaches that meaning comes only from awareness of experience; Perls taught awareness for its own sake.

Contemporary life in the United States and much of the western world can be described in terms of relative peace and prosperity, and the immediate prognosis is for more of the same. The search for meaning and the wish for emotional survival continues. The promise of existential philosophy is being actively examined by many, and those who have experienced the Gestalt approach to the discovery of personal awareness believe that the means for achieving meaningful existence has been found.

Assumptions

More will be said later of theoretical assumptions regarding existentialism in the form of Gestalt therapy and for this reason only a brief overview is presented here. The following fundamental assumptions are discussed more fully by Beck (1963), Hall and Lindzey (1970), Patterson (1966), and Shertzer and Stone (1974).

Existentialists believe that behavior is an expression of present awareness and nothing more. It is not determined by, nor is it an extension of, innate drives, environmental variables, or prior experience. An individual can discover and act on his or her awareness at any given moment within certain limits imposed by physical, cultural, and other environmental factors. It appears that most existentialists recognize the place of learning; that is, client behavior is regarded as learned actions considered appropriate for the goals and directions he or she has determined.

Regarding the predictability of client behavior, a concern among many approaches to counseling, existentialists and Gestaltists regard the matter as irrelevant. Client behavior cannot be predicted (Why would anyone want to?) since we all have the capacity to alter directions and choices at all times. The major dynamic in counseling and therapy is behavior change. Existentialists share this goal and explain that it will occur when the client chooses to do so and the counselor facilitates this by doing whatever will assist the client in being more fully aware of his or her existence (feelings, thoughts, fantasies, wishes, values, etc.).

The ways in which joy, the avowed goal of Gestalt Therapy, can be achieved vary from one person to another. While it is true that several techniques have become identified with the Gestalt approach it is also true that the number of ways in which one person can be facilitative with another seems almost infinite.

Summary

During the past century there have been six relatively distinct stages in the evolution of assumptions regarding the nature of man and in counseling theories, assumptions and methods. Prior to the turn of the century, human behavior was nature's greatest mystery and there seemed to be little that one person could do for another in relation to emotional dilemmas. Counseling and therapy in their present forms were nonexistent and any help with personal problems consisted largely of listening, trying to understand, and urging compliance with whatever conditions were prevalent. Any need for assistance was often regarded as a deviation, a weakness, or resistance in accepting nature's basic processes.

Freud opened an entirely new universe of human experience, the mind and its workings. He not only established that there was reason and order at the heart of thought and feeling processes but also continued throughout his lifetime to find and demonstrate ways of changing behavior. The legacy of Freud and others who have followed in the field of analytic psychology is massive and invaluable. In addition to developing and refining the entire field of applied psychology they passed down several methodological artifacts including focused listening, the importance of early experience, the clinical interview, hypnosis, free association, dream interpretation, and insight, to name only a few.

We have both the pioneers and settlers in the trait and factor approach to thank for all that has been learned of appraisal and diagnosis. Surely this approach can take credit as well for grasping the significance of such systematic procedures as goal-setting, evaluation and reevaluation of counseling progress, assessing movement toward goals and using various forms of information in counseling. From a heritage consisting of analytic psychology and measurement, the proponents of this approach have evolved an objective, rational, and outcome-based approach.

The phenomenologists, notably Carl Rogers, have provided an authentic new definition of reality that had largely eluded their predecessors. Rogers' discovery of subjective reality as the ultimate criterion in counseling and therapy has revolutionized not only the theoretical assumptions upon which counseling is predicated but has also produced, or at least contributed to, an entirely new variety of counseling and therapy techniques. The client-centered approach with its emphasis upon acceptance, positive regard, and an enabling relationship has shifted the focus in counselor training from a cognitive understanding of behavior to a sensitive, empathic experiencing of it. This new perspective has done much to influence the training and practice of counselors and therapists of all theoretical persuasions and has been a cornerstone in the establishment of humanistic psychology, a major social revolution of the current era.

Those who espouse the learning and behaviorism approach to counseling have succeeded in demonstrating beyond any shadow of a doubt that specific behaviors can be changed without reliance upon a comprehensive view of the nature of man, other than simply understanding that behavior is learned. At a time when so many are sure of so little, other than that they wish to behave differently, the emergence of an approach to counseling that can demonstrate observable outcomes is highly propitious. Capitalizing upon the appropriate elements of counseling from earlier periods regarding the importance of a healthy counselor-client relationship, the usefulness of information, specific focus and a systematic procedure, the behaviorists have developed methods for applying the fundamentals of learning to behavior change in counseling and therapy. Much of what was seen only dimly before is now clear; what was thought impossible can now be accomplished.

The existentialists behind the banner of Perls and other Gestaltists have, like Rogers, developed an approach to counseling based exclusively upon the client's awareness of reality. Some have noted the high degree of philosophical similarity and point out that Gestalt therapy is most importantly different in regard to method and technique. Certainly the Gestalt approach has provided hitherto unknown strategies for facilitating client awareness in a more active means rather than simply trusting that such new perceptions will emerge. The emphases upon contact, present experiencing including sensory as well as cognitive and affective awareness, remembering, rehearsing, and discontinuing the sanity-insanity dilemma have contributed bright, exciting new vistas. In the Gestalt approach the counselor's goal is to facilitate client discovery of his or her awareness based upon the counselor's experiencing (rather than understanding) of the client.

2

Gestalt Theory

It was noted in Chapter 1 that Gestalt psychotherapy is a relative newcomer to the therapeutic scene in America. Only in the past ten to fifteen years have the helping professions reflected the powerful influence of Gestalt thinking and practice. Even now, the Gestalt approach is viewed by many as exciting, highly promising and new. However, the thinking on which Gestalt psychotherapy is based has been with us for a much longer period of time, stretching back even into the past century in some cases.

Gestalt psychotherapy has drawn on three distinctly different sources for its rationale, principles, and assumptions. The first, and obvious source, is Gestalt learning theory. Many of the principles and assumptions that were explored by Koffka, Köhler, Wertheimer, and Lewin have been borrowed by Gestalt counseling psychologists and applied to human development. A second source of influence in Gestalt psychotherapy, as we know it in America, has been Freudian psychoanalytic thinking. Through the influence of Freud, as well as contact with Otto Rank and Wilhelm Reich, Frederick Perls incorporated classical psychoanalytic thinking into a contemporary Gestalt psychotherapy. Finally, European existential thought has contributed many philosophical threads to the Gestalt garment. In order to better understand the complexities of Gestalt therapeutic theory, it would be helpful to examine these sources in greater detail.

Gestalt as a Learning Theory

The Gestalt approach to psychology had its origins in Germany in the first quarter of the twentieth century. Its introduction to American scholars occurred with the publication of Kurt Koffka's *Growth of the Mind* (1924), and Wolfgang Köhler's *Mentality of Apes* (1925). The publication of these works coincided with the first visits to America by both of these German scholars. As fate would have it, American psychology at the time was involved in an academic struggle between scholars variously labeled structuralists, functionalists, and behaviorists, and scholars who had no rallying point. The basic quarrel of the day appeared to be whether or not the human being was a thinking, learning organism, or according to Hilgard (1956, p. 224), merely "played upon by the pushes and pulls of the environment, [reacting] in ways essentially stupid." Köhler's work with apes and Koffka's theses both proposed a strong alternative, rather naively labeled "insight." Nonetheless, it was this alternative position that many American psychologists had been waiting for and the result was like seeds finding fertile ground.

Some of the more important concepts that Gestalt theory has contributed are the *law of Prägnanz,* which in turn incorporated the laws of similarity, proximity, closure, and good continuation. Wallen (1970, p. 8) has noted that "the academic Gestalt psychologist never attempted to employ [these principles] to organic perceptions, to the perceptions of one's own feelings, emotions, and bodily sensations." Nevertheless, later psychologists, notably Frederick Perls, did show how these principles have direct application to human emotions.

The law of *Prägnanz* suggests a predisposition to move in a specific direction rather than random movement. In its relationship to human beings, it can be thought of as a law of psychological equilibrium, a tendency for the organism to return to a state of balance at times when the organism experiences imbalance, either through emotional stress, learning demand, or other psychological effect.

Koffka developed four additional laws, each of which seemed to illustrate in its own way the law of *Prägnanz*. The first of these was the law of similarity. This law states that similar items or events tend to be united in one's perception. That is, as we perceive events, people, objects, our perceptions lead naturally to similarities rather than dissimilarities.

The second law is the *law of proximity*. Simply stated, this law states that when one perceives objects or events, those which are proximally close to one another are perceived as clusters. Numerous Gestalt experiments using several parallel lines, some spaced evenly apart, others unevenly, have demonstrated this principle. Hilgard (1956, p. 228) notes that as this law "applies to memory, [it] becomes a law of recency. Old impressions are less well-recognized and recalled than new ones."

The *law of closure* is Koffka's third contribution. It speaks to the organism's need to realize completeness when incompleteness exists. It presumes that unclosed situations are less stable than are closed ones. In human interactions this law achieves high significance. It applies to incomplete interactions, partially realized emotions, and so forth. We shall see later that the law of closure holds a dominant place in Gestalt therapy.

The fourth law is that of *good continuation*. This law, like the others, is related to perceptual processes rather than internal processes. It says that when we see a partial circle, we will extend the line to see it as a full circle. Or, a broken straight line will be seen as a continuous straight line. This concept can be applied to the perception of events, and in this sense, has relevance for human development. For example, if person A responds in a certain way to anxiety two times out of every three, person B might operate on the law of good continuation to say that person A *always* reacts that way to anxiety.

The final contribution of Gestalt learning theory that we shall discuss is also the most consequential.The early Gestalt experiments of Köhler and Gottschaldt dealt specifically with perception of figures in space. These included pictures of multiple parallel lines, arrangements of small boxes in larger boxes, pictures of geometric figures that appeared to have three-dimensional qualities, etc. These experiments were all used to study what Rubin referred to as the "figure-ground." Köhler (1947, p. 202) describes it in this way:

> Since an area becomes solid when it has shape, and is in this sense a figure, Rubin has given the solid quality the name "figure character." He calls the looseness of the environment the "ground character." The term "ground" is particularly appropriate because the figure generally

protrudes a bit in space. The unshaped environment is localized further backward, and actually seems to extend behind the figure as a homogeneous plane on which the figure lies.

The concept of the figure-ground has unique applications in Gestalt therapy, as we shall see later. As a result of focusing upon that part of the design that offers closure, the focused element emerges as the more dominant part of the total picture. And as it emerges, other elements of the picture recede, perceptually, into the background (ground). So it is with human experiences. In any given event, the stimuli of the environmental setting are far greater than the human mind can absorb and classify. As a result, we learn to focus our attention on those stimuli that possess the qualities of good configuration, closure, proximity, similarity, or *Prägnanz*. In other words, we filter out much that is part of the experience in order to comprehend the experience. It is this emotional perception process that Gestalt psychotherapy has drawn from Gestalt learning theory.

Freudian Traces in Gestalt Psychotherapy

It is virtually impossible to speak of Gestalt therapy without speaking of the Freudian effect on Gestalt thinking. The relationship between the two theories is manifested in the personage of Frederick (Fritz) Perls. Perls is widely acknowledged as the most formidable force in the conceptualization of Gestalt psychotherapy. His training occurred at a time when Freud was the dominant psychiatric figure in Europe. As fate will sometimes have it, that training led him to Wilhelm Reich, one of Freud's early students. Reich became Perls' teacher and analyst* and had a profound effect upon him.

Time and again in his writings, Perls used Freud as his touchstone when making a point. Typically these references spoke to Perls' disagreement with Freud and did so with such frequency that one could begin to wonder what was the underlying issue between them. Perls did speak to this question in one of his later writings (1969b, p. 45):

> Many friends criticize me for my polemic relationship to Freud. "You have so much to say; your position is securely grounded in reality. What is this continuous aggressiveness against Freud? Leave him alone and just do your thing."

* One must remember that Perls was in training to be a psychoanalyst. Part of that training involved his own analysis.

> I can't do this. Freud, his theories, his influence are much too important for me. My admiration, bewilderment, and vindictiveness are very strong. I am deeply moved by his suffering and courage. I am deeply awed by how much, practically all alone, he achieved with the inadequate mental tools of association-psychology and mechanistically-oriented philosophy. I am deeply grateful for how much I developed through standing up against him.

There is little doubt that Perls' formulations were often times provoked by his reactions to Freud's thoughts. For the most part, Perls thought that Freud had missed the essence of the therapeutic experience. Yet Perls did concur with certain elements of Freud's theories and adopt them, with modifications, into his own thinking. Fagan and Shepherd (1970, p. 4) have identified two such contributions: "[Freud's] idea of the unconscious, which Perls translates as describing those aspects of behavior that are unavailable or potential rather than actual; and the concept of thinking as trial work or rehearsing, leading to the Gestalt therapy formulation of anxiety as stage fright." There also appears to be a third concept significant enough to merit acknowledgement. That is Perls' treatment of dreams. While there are very specific points of disagreement between Perls and Freud on what to do with dreams, Perls is in essential agreement with Freud on the significance of dream content and the need to deal with dreams as a part of therapy. Let us consider each of these three contributions in greater detail.

It could be said that Perls' concept of rehearsal was only an oblique reference to Freud's earlier work. Indeed, Perls felt that Freud never did follow up on his own idea to its logical conclusion. Nonetheless, the idea of rehearsal is significant, both to Freud and Perls. Rehearsal is an act that takes place in the conscious. It includes activities such as planning, remembering, speculating, anticipating, and creating expectations. In a word, rehearsing is *thinking*. Perls described it as a "private stage on which we prepare for the future roles we want to play." He saw it as talking to "someone unknown, [talking] to yourself, [preparing] for an important event, [talking] to your beloved before your appointment or disappointment, whatever you expect it to be [1969a, p. 59]."*

Freud placed emphasis more upon the effect of rehearsal anxiety. He summarized it in this way (1936, p. 112): "Anxiety is undeniably related to expectation; one feels anxiety *lest* something occur." In a

*From Frederick S. Perls, *Gestalt Therapy Verbatim,* p. 59, and elsewhere pp. 47, 50, 51, 53, 54, 60. Copyright 1969 by Real People Press, Moab, Utah. Reprinted by permission of the publisher.

more specific way, he viewed rehearsal anxiety as neurotic anxiety, a danger which we do not know. Freud's prescription was to bring this danger of which the ego was unaware into consciousness, thus reducing it to "true anxiety" which was more "treatable."

For Perls the relevance of rehearsal was not just the act of anticipation. Perls viewed its purpose as the attempt to cope with anxiety; anxiety experienced in the "now" but related to the future. He noted that there are "few people who can stand this tension, so they have to fill the gap with rehearsing, planning, 'making sure,' making sure that they don't have a future [1969a, p. 51]." Thus, we could say that for Freud, rehearsal was an attempt to deal with the future, while for Perls, it was an attempt to avoid the future.

We shall turn now to Freud's second major contribution, the unconscious. Freud viewed the unconscious as that large inaccessible portion of the mind, similar to the submerged portion of an iceberg. He saw it as "a special realm, with its own desires and modes of expression and peculiar mental mechanisms not elsewhere operative [1960, p. 222]." The unconscious appears to be its own master and serves as the repository for those mental processes that are usually the causes of human actions.

Perls liked Freud's conception of the unconscious. But he chose to interpret its significance differently than did Freud. According to Perls (1970, p. 16):

> Freud said (this is not his formulation, but my understanding of what he meant) that in a neurosis a part of our personality or of our potential is not available. But he said this in an odd way; he said, "it is *in* the unconscious," as if there were such a thing as *the* unconscious rather than simply behavior or emotions that are unknown or not available.

Perls viewed the unconscious more as a barrier between the person and his or her lost potential. The Gestalt objective is to lift the barrier, thus permitting the person once again to become totally him/herself. Perls posited that this is done through the integration of attention and awareness on those areas that are blocked from awareness.

The third Freudian concept that has found its way into Gestalt thinking and practice is the treatment of dreams. The point can be made that dreams constitute part of the unconscious. However, Gestalt thinking and treatment of dream content are significantly different from the Freudian position that justifies the treatment of dreams as a separate entity. Freud proposed that the content of dreams is somehow derived from experience, but acknowledged that the link between dreams and reality was a very difficult one to make. Only through repeated examination of dreams is one likely to recognize a pattern that leads to understanding and insight (1953). This reflects Freud's reluctance to accept the obvious content of dreams. For him, dreams were filled with symbolism that led to deeper, more significant meanings.

Perls was inclined to agree. As was typical of him, his agreement was with his interpretation of Freud more than with Freud's words, however. His acknowledgement of the dream concept reflects this.

> Freud's beautiful distinction between the "manifest" and the "latent" dream means precisely that the dreaming consciousness is isolated from *both* the environment and the organism; the "self" that the dreamer is aware of is largely *merely* the surface-boundary [1951].

While both believed that dreams contained the material of inner conflict, they did not agree on how that material should be treated. As was mentioned earlier, Freud interpreted the symbolism of the dreams to the dreamer. Perls disavowed interpretation as a tool because it robbed the dreamer of the opportunity to establish his own meaning. Instead, Perls would have the client re-enact or live out the dream, or even several characters in the dream. This would be done in a role play with the therapist acting as director rather than participant.

The Existential Elements in Gestalt Therapy

Perls quarrels with existentialism in much the same way that he quarrelled with Freud. Yet he also uses existential thinking as a springboard to clarify his thinking. Much of his reference to existentialism is in an effort to show how the existentialists have fallen short of their goal, that a thing can be explained through its very existence. One could get the impression that existential thought failed to influence Gestalt therapy because of this shortcoming. Such does not appear to be the case, as Enright and others have observed (1970). We shall speak further to this point later.

Another philosophical thread is laced through Perls' writing and thinking. That is the Zen Buddhist or Eastern philosophies. For purposes of our investigation into philosophical bases of Gestalt, we shall treat Zen as a parallel to existentialism. Rollo May has made the same comparisons.

> One gets the . . . shock of similarity in Zen Buddhism. The likeness between these Eastern philosophies and existentialism goes much deeper than the chance similarity of words. Both are concerned with ontology, the study of being. Both seek a relation to reality which cuts

> below the cleavage between subject and object. Both would insist that the Western absorption in conquering and gaining power over nature has resulted not only in the estrangement of man from nature but also indirectly in the estrangement of man from himself. The basic reason for these similarities is that Eastern thought never suffered the radical split between subject and object that has characterized Western thought, and this dichotomy is exactly what existentialism seeks to overcome [1970, p. 18–19].

Perls picks up this thread several times in his writing: ". . . in Gestalt therapy we try to be consistent with every other event, especially with nature because we are a part of nature." At another point, he observes, "Gestalt therapy is a philosophy that tries to be in harmony, in alignment with everything else, with medicine, with science, with the universe, with what is [1970, p. 16–17]."

Being "in tune with nature" is primarily related to the Gestalt concept of awareness and present-centeredness. It is at this point that the Zen effect and the existential effect converge. Laura Perls acknowledges this convergence as it relates to the very real existential issues of living and death.

> In the East, the aim of Zen Buddhism is precisely this realization of identity of living and dying, of commitment and detachment. In our Western world, the neurotic is the man who cannot face his own dying and therefore cannot live fully as a human being. Gestalt therapy, with its emphasis on immediate awareness and involvement, offers a method for developing the necessary support for a self-continuing creative adjustment — which is the only way of coping with the experience of dying and, therefore, of living [1970, p. 129].

This "in-tune-ness" with the self and nature is the unifying concept that ties together the several philosophical and psychological sources of Gestalt theory. As we shall see later, it is evident in the layers of neurosis that Perls uses to describe progress in therapy. It is the inherent goal of this basic technique of confrontation. It is the ultimate objective of the Gestaltist.

The Application of Gestalt Theory

The two fundamental concepts of Gestalt psychotherapy are the *organism* and the *environment.* They are unique from one another and yet they are inseparable. They are the equivalent of the Gestalt psychologist's figure-ground. The organism is the person, the individual. Perls refers to it as two people: the public person and the private person. It is the whole person. Where other therapies focus upon the "thinking person" or the "feeling person," Gestalt attempts to account for the total gestalt. If we think of the person as a highly complex system of interwoven physiological and psychological functions that are in constant interaction with one another and with the environment, we are then approaching the concept of the organism.

The environment is all that is external to the organism. It has been referred to as the person's world, his/her perceptions, his/her reality. It is composed of other organisms, objects, events, processes. We have said that the organism and its environment are unique, yet inseparable. This is so because the organism is in constant contact and interaction with the environment. It is impossible to describe the organism's functioning without also including the environment within which it functions. Perls, Hefferline, and Goodman (1951, p. 228) describe it by pointing out that

> It makes no sense to speak . . . of an animal that breathes without considering air and oxygen as part of its definition, or to speak of eating without mentioning food, or of seeing without light, or locomotion without gravity and supporting ground, or of speech without communicants. There is no single function of any animal that completes itself without objects and environment.

This interaction which incorporates the organism and its environment is referred to as the *organism/environment field.* It is important to note that the field is both physical and social. It is our total world.

The organism/environment field encompasses all that we experience. These experiences occur at that point where organism and environment meet; that point is referred to as the *organism/environment contact boundary.* If we walk out of a warm room into a cold winter day, our skin experiences the change in temperature by tingling. In this example, the contact boundary is that interaction between skin and cold air. It is this region at which experiencing occurs. Gestaltists refer to this as the region of growth. When experience bursts into our awareness, we have increased the "in-tune-ness" with self and nature to which we referred earlier.

One of the maladies most of us suffer to some degree is sensory dullness. Sensory dullness can range from a deadened sense of taste or smell to the more social dullnesses that characterize human non-relationships. Sensory dullness in any form leads toward the same end. It tends to deny our existence, our living, feeling, experiencing selves. Eating a gourmet meal can be a living excitement or it can be noticed only in its final effect, the filled stomach. In a more social sense, we can live most of any day by noticing and experiencing the richness of our fellow companions, or we can isolate ourselves and experience life as a grey existence. Parents often get caught up in this trap and realize only too late that they have missed experiencing the joys of their children's childhoods.

It becomes apparent that the key to growth in the region of the organism/environment contact boundary is *awareness.* Without awareness, social and physical sensory dullness set in, and we miss the experiencing of our lives, the actual events that establish our living existence.

Perls refers to awareness as covering three layers or three zones. These zones are awareness of the self; awareness of the world; and "awareness of what's between — the intermediate zone of fantasy that prevents a person from being in touch with either himself or the world [1969a, p. 53]." Perls describes this intermediate zone as a place where many processes operate. He cites prejudice as an example (p. 53). "If you have prejudices, then your relationship to the word is very much disturbed and destroyed. If you want to approach a person with a prejudice, you can't get to the person. You always will contact only the prejudice, the fixed idea." All of us have this intermediate zone of fantasy. As with the other layers of awareness our fantasies can be creative assets if we experience them in the *now*. When experienced in the *now*, they produce a healthy state of spontaneity. Perls speaks to this process: "In the *now*, you use what is available, and you are bound to be creative. Just watch children in their play. What's available is usable and then something happens, something comes out of the being in touch with what is *here* and *now* [p. 54]."

The concepts of *now* and *how* are unique to the pursuit of awareness. *Now* means this moment, the only moment that holds the potential for experiencing. *Now* is all that we have. All that precedes this moment is gone. We cannot recover any of our past. We can relive our past, but if we choose to do that, we are living in the intermediate zone of fantasy that prevents us from being in touch with ourselves or our world. (This is not to suggest that in the practice of Gestalt therapy, the past is ignored. On the contrary, material out of the client's past is used, but the attempt is made to bring it into the present as it affects the *now*.)

How provides the structure of our experience in the *now*. Perls describes it as "all we need to understand how we or the world functions. The *how* gives us perspective, orientation. The *how* shows that one of the basic laws, the identity of structure and function, is valid. If we change the structure, the function changes. If we change the function, the structure changes. *How* covers everything that is structure, behavior, all that is actually going on —

the ongoing process. All the rest is irrelevant — computing, apprehending, and so on [1969a, p. 47]."

Thus we have the person (organism-in-its-environment) striving to experience his/her environment in the present moment of existence. That experiencing occurs and awareness develops at the organism/environment contact boundary. Perls conceptualized the contact as the *how*, the structure of the experience. From a theoretical view, contact may be conceptualized as the formation of a *figure* of interest against a *ground* or context of the organism/environment field. The figure is specifically psychological. That is, according to Perls, Hefferline, and Goodman (1951, p. 231–232),

> . . . it has specific observable properties of brightness, clarity, unity, fascination, grace, vigor, release, etc. (which provides) an autonomous criterion of the depth and reality of the experience. In a weak gestalt, there is lack of contact, something is blocked out, some need is not expressed. A strong gestalt is itself the cure, for the figure of contact is itself the creative integration of experience.

Earlier we noted the importance of the law of *Prägnanz* to Gestalt theory. It states that the human organism has a tendency to return to a state of balance at times when it experiences imbalance, either through emotional stress, learning demand, or other psychological effect. From a Gestalt therapy viewpoint, these stresses and demands produce or lead to the experiencing of needs. Functionally, as the individual becomes aware of and begins to attend to these needs, he or she returns to a state of equilibrium. What follows is a fairly simplistic statement of the nature of mental health. The healthy person is one who experiences his or her needs at their moment of emergence, and by attending to those felt needs, returns to his or her natural state of balance or equilibrium. The difficulty is not in *how* one maintains a healthy organism. It springs from interferences to this process. It is the *what* of the process rather than the *how*.

Wallen (1970) notes three kinds of interference that prevent or impede the organism in its response to the law of *Prägnanz*. The first of these is poor perceptual contact with the external world and with the body itself. This is found in patients who cannot make or maintain eye contact with the therapist or with objects they are trying to describe. They may be unaware of movements of their own bodies, such as clenched fists, arms tightly clutching their chests, or voices that are inconsistent with or contradict their verbal message. Such insensitivity to one's body or to one's surroundings would produce an obvious block to the emergence of felt needs.

A second interference comes when the open expression of needs is blocked.

> For example, the patient may feel some warmth but not be able to do anything about it. Since the patient does not express his needs, he actually never gets the satisfaction for them; a perceptual figure that could have been bright, unified, and meaningful becomes dull and uninteresting, and the need thus actually never gets discharged. Consider somebody with a need for affection that is only half expressed. Half satisfaction results because the need is never thoroughly discharged. This particular need then serves to energize parts of the perceptual field; the person is looking for affection but not really wholeheartedly. The end result is that the need continues interfering with other kinds of needs that might organize the field in a clear-cut and coherent way [p. 11].

The third source of interference that prevents the formation of good gestalts is repression. Wallen points out that the Gestalt therapist's view of the nature of repression can be traced back to Wilhelm Reich (who was Frederick Perls' analyst). Repression is treated as a muscular phenomenon.

> Thus when needs and impulses arise, there tends to be a muscular response. The response tends to play itself out on the motor level, and the only way that one can inhibit the response is by contracting antagonistic muscles that prevent this impulse from expressing itself fully. The simplest example would be an impulse to swear at somebody. Let us suppose that you are very angry and yet you have to hold the impulse back. Now this holding back process can be seen as a strictly muscular process. There are contractions in the jaws; there are tensions in the arm that prevent, for example, shaking the fist. In the case of sadness, the normal postural responses if the need played itself out thoroughly would be dejected posture, drawn mouth, and empty face. In holding sadness back, the simplest alteration would be to push the lips upward into a smile, destroying the pattern associated with sadness and thus not expressing and discharging the emotion [p. 12].

These muscular reactions that serve to repress the physical expression of feelings tend to become habitual responses. As a result we adapt to them and lose the awareness that we are blocking an emotion or even what the emotion is that we are blocking.

Whether the source of interference be poor perceptual contact with oneself or the world, the open expression of needs, or repression, the Gestalt therapist's prescription is the same: awareness. Again, a deceptively simple statement emerges. The remedy for blocks to awareness is awareness of the blocks. In a more practical sense, Enright (1970) has identified four ways in which we block awareness. These are retroflection, desensitization, introjection, and projection. He notes that each functions from moment to moment in the "here and now" to block awareness of current behavior, "or as repetitive residuals of earlier attempts to avoid awareness [p. 111]."

The first of these, retroflection, is, according to Enright,

> the general process of negating, holding back, or balancing the impulse tension by additional, opposing sensorimotor tension. The concept includes most of what is often referred to as repression and inhibition, and emphasizes the *how* of the processes involved. Since the net result of all this canceled-out muscular tension is zero — no overt movement — there is no particular increase in activity at the contact boundary, and awareness does not develop. Later, perhaps, since there is increased activity at the points of muscular opposition, awareness may develop there as pain or discomfort. This process of retroflection can be transitory or chronic. The cry of distress begins with moistening the eyes and a characteristic facial expression; the "stiff upper lip" and the literal holding (squeezing) back of tears constitute the retroflection. This can last a moment before the tears break through or a lifetime [p. 112].

Projection is a more active process. It occurs when an individual is unable to "own" or acknowledge aspects of his or her own personality or behavior. Instead, he or she attributes these qualities or behaviors to others and becomes highly critical of minor manifestations of these qualities in the other person. The Gestalt therapist does not attribute projection to unconscious forces as does the Freudian therapist. Rather, he or she sees projection as a conscious process, albeit a process that is marked by lack of awareness.

Enright states that desensitization is "the sensory analog to motoric retroflection. Scotomata, visual blurring, chronic 'not hearing', sensory dullness, frigidity, etc., are equal in importance to retroflection in the blocking of awareness. They are, however, more dependent on verbal report and hence less accessible to direct observation and study than motoric phenomena [p. 112]."

The fourth block of awareness described by Enright is introjection. Introjections are "adopted" behaviors. They "consist of complex, integrated ways of behaving or being [acquired] by the developing organism from significant others *without assimilation or integration with the self.* They can be detected by the repeated concurrence of a certain voice quality, type of verbal content and gesture-posture style, and by the similarity with which others respond to this unified complex of behavior [p. 112]." Introjections reflect the individual's lack of awareness or understanding of self. They represent what Enright calls the "endless self-nagging and inner argument between the 'ideal' and 'real' self in which so many people fritter away their lives [p. 113]."

The major effect of blocks to awareness is that gestalts are never formed for the individual. Needs are only partially experienced and therefore only partially met. Much unfinished business accumulates. The individual may develop phobias, obsessions, or anxiety. Life becomes very uninteresting. The transformation from living to existing is made. Enright notes that often the patient "has successfully distracted himself from even knowing where he hurts, and his 'problem' or 'presenting complaint' is not the meaningful place to start therapy [p. 113]."

The process of therapy consists of the identification and "working through" of these blocks, opening up the individual's experiencing so that needs can be experienced, acted upon or acted out, and gestalts completed. There are stages or layers that the patient passes through as this process gets enacted. These are referred to by Perls as the "five layers of neurosis," and include the *cliche layer*, the *phony layer*, the *impasse*, the *implosive layer*, and the *explosive layer*.

Perls believed that most of us operate in the cliche and phony layers. The cliche layer is as it sounds, a pattern of non-contact with others or with ideas, events, experiences. It is the "Hello, how are you today?" "I am fine, thank you, and how are you?" kinds of experiences. The cliche layer is the beginning point, and the "safest" point of all relationships, because it is the point of almost total non-committal. Also, it is a layer that is easily passed through because one can move from it into the almost equally safe phony or game-playing layer.

Perls liked to call this second layer the Eric Berne or Sigmund Freud layer. It is "the layer where we play games and roles — the very important person, the bully, the cry-baby, the nice little girl, the good boy — whatever roles we choose to play. [They] are the superficial, social, *as-if* layers. We pretend to be better, tougher, weaker, more polite, etc., than we really feel [Perls, 1969a, p. 59]." People live most of their lives in this layer. Indeed, Perls believed that most approaches to therapy spent themselves in the phony layer. For to get beyond the game-playing is to get beyond the roles that we use to establish our identities with ourselves.

Without the roles of our daily lives, we are thrust into the impasse layer. There "we experience the *anti*-existence, we experience the nothingness, emptiness. This is . . . the feeling of being stuck and lost. The impasse is marked by a phobic attitude — avoidance. We are phobic, we are suffering, especially the suffering of frustration [p. 60]." There is an exercise that often illustrates quite well the impasse and its consequence, the implosive layer. The exercise, called role-stripping, calls upon the participant to identify and write down his or her most important role, be it father, mother, student, lover, son or daughter, or business person. Then the second most important role, third most important, fourth most important, and fifth most important are identified and written down. This simple process of identifying and writing down these very significant roles is often very revealing for participants. The next step is a fantasy trip. The participant is asked to give up his or her fifth role and to imagine what life would be like without it. The same is done with each succeeding role until the most important role has to be relinquished. Even in a fantasy experience, the trauma that the participant experiences in giving up these roles is visible and dramatic.

The consequence of giving up one's roles is called the implosive layer. This fourth layer appears either as death or as fear of death. Since we have given up the roles that gave us our identities, we no longer have identities. We are non-beings. We are forced to look into ourselves in our search for who we are. We must come up with new definitions of self, definitions that reflect personhood rather than role. Perls refers to this layer as

> . . . a kind of catatonic paralysis: we pull ourselves together, we contract and compress ourselves, we *implode*.
>
> The *im*plosion becomes *ex*plosion. The death layer comes to life, and this explosion is the link-up with the authentic person who is capable of experiencing and expressing his emotions. There are four basic kinds of explosions from the death layer. There is the explosion of genuine *grief* if we work through a loss or death that has not been assimilated. There is the explosion into *orgasm* in sexually blocked people. There is the explosion into *anger*, and also the explosion into *joy, laughter, joi de vivre*. These explosions connect with the authentic personality, with the true self [1969a, p. 60].

It is often difficult for the person newly introduced to Gestalt therapy to comprehend the passage through impasse and implosion, to explosion. Such experiences rarely happen in most people's everyday living. Yet all of us have, at one time or another, reached that soul-searching depth which led to our getting in touch with values and self-perceptions that form the core of our existence. The process is best understood only after it has been experienced.

It is this explosion into life, living, experiencing people, events, and needs, acting and responding spontaneously, permitting the authentic self to live that Gestalt therapy seeks to establish for the patient. Nested within this object is the assumption that we are best for ourselves when we *are* ourselves.

As in many other therapeutic approaches, the fundamental goal of Gestalt therapy is the search for the authentic self. There are numerous methods that the Gestalt therapist uses to help guide the patient through the maze of his or her defenses toward that goal. We shall discuss methods and techniques in detail in Chapter 3. However, there is one aspect of this process that merits discussion here, particularly within the context of its theoretical implications. We refer to the Gestalt treatment of dreams. One must acknowledge Freud's influence on Gestalt thinking, since there is no reference either in existential thought or Gestalt psychology to the relationship between dreams and the "real self."

You will recall that Freud believed dreams to be the most direct access to the unconscious. In his treatment of patients, he encouraged them to remember and describe their dreams. He saw dreams as being rich in symbolism, offering many cues to the patient's earlier fixations or impeded psychological development. Freud rarely responded to the immediacy of the dream description. Rather, he waited and watched for recurring patterns or themes to emerge. Then he would offer his interpretation of the meaning of the patient's trauma, referring to the data gained in the dreams to support his conclusions.

Perls treated dreams quite differently. He saw them as having a direct link to the patient's spontaneous or "real" self. They did not reflect the unconscious, in a Freudian sense. Instead they reflected unintegrated realities or experience. Perls used the content of dreams in the immediate moment of their description. Like Freud, he saw dreams as being saturated with symbols. Unlike Freud, he asked the patient to interpret the symbols, to find the relevance, to locate the self that was represented in the dream. In fact, Perls believed that it was always a therapeutic mistake for the therapist to offer interpretation to the patient. This interpretation that the patient was called upon to make occurred through the re-enactment or role-playing of different parts of the dream. We shall discuss the treatment of dreams in more detail later.

Summary

We began in our considerations of Gestalt therapy by looking to those sources and antecedents that have been major contributors to the approach. These include Gestalt learning theory, existentialism and Zen Buddhism, and Sigmund Freud, his thinking, theorizing, and his student, Wilhelm Reich.

Gestalt learning theory contributed the law of *Prägnanz,* the effect of which can be seen in the Gestalt view of the healthy organism. Similarly, the laws of proximity, similarity, closure, and good continuation may be seen as contributing to the formation of gestalts as the individual grows in awareness.

Existentialism and Zen Buddhism are reflected in the concept of self, the trauma of nothingness that is experienced in the impasse, and the implosion that becomes the search for self.

Finally, we have traced the influence and effect Sigmund Freud had upon Frederick Perls, the most significant contributor to Gestalt therapy. Perls loved and hated Freud's effect. He chafed under Freud's restrictive perceptions. Yet he freely acknowledged Freud as the person who most challenged his own thinking.

The second half of this chapter has examined the details of Gestalt therapy. Beginning with the organism-in-its-environment, we briefly examined the nature of that organism/environment relationship. The transactions that occur are heavily dependent in their impact upon the individual's level of awareness. Awareness and attentiveness incorporate the self, the world, and an inner zone of fantasy. Often environmental contacts are incomplete as a result of blocks to awareness. These lead to incomplete gestalts, unfulfilled needs, and unfinished business. As this process compounds itself, the individual experiences greater anxiety, phobic reactions and obsessions.

The therapeutic process that retrieves the patient from this lost potential involves the passage through five layers of neurosis. These layers include the cliche layer, the phony, game-playing layer, the impasse, implosion, and explosion into authentic existence and awareness. In Chapter 3 we shall examine the techniques of therapy that permit this process to occur.

3

Methods and Techniques

The ability to reason is both the agony and the joy of being human. This is the ultimate paradox of the human experience, and countless volumes have been written concerning its resolution. The capacity of cognitive awareness is at one time a gift of incomparable ecstasy and at other times an unrelenting curse. Needless to say, we often don't know what to make of it. Having the ability to wonder, we wonder. Our wonderings are conceptualized and expressed in words which are used as symbols of actual experience. It is in this process, according to existentialists, that the joy of the human experience gets lost. Gestaltists believe that important origins of neurosis or simple unhappiness can be attributed to the abilities of thinking and communicating. Other approaches to counseling rely either heavily or exclusively upon the capacity for thinking either to resolve the entire mystery of the human experience or at least to solve some of the difficulties that arise during the process.

In the Gestalt approach the aim of counseling and therapy is to take advantage of all dimensions of humanness by achieving an integration of the thinking, feeling and sensing processes. The goal is to enable full experiencing rather than merely a cognitive understanding of certain elements.

The following discussion of how our use of language and thinking can lead to insanity (non-being) was written two years ago by Charles Mowrer, a Purdue University doctoral student. We believe that he has provided a highly useful description of the difference between thinking and experiencing, one that has clear relevance for this chapter devoted to the methods and techniques of the Gestalt approach to counseling. His brief personal account of discovering, experiencing, and integrating both processes is particularly appropriate.

LANGUAGE AND INSANITY*

Charles W. Mowrer

My conceptualization of the mechanism of insanity began in an unlikely place, a science fiction novel entitled *The World of Null-A,* by A. W. Van Vogt. Besides being an imaginative little science fiction novel, it proved to contain some new concepts (for me) which caused some thought. Van Vogt postulated a future in A.D. 2560 where sanity was gradually becoming the norm rather than the abnormal. This is not to say that insanity does not exist in his future. In fact, much of the story is about the protagonist's (the epitome of the null-A person) efforts to save the developing neophyte sane world from destruction by galactic and earth forces that were characterized as insane. But this is beside the point; what interested me was Van Vogt's conceptualization of how the antagonists were distinguished.

Van Vogt borrowed Alfred Korzybski's ideas and used them as a base for his novel. For Van Vogt the ultimate in sanity is the null-A thinker, or the non-Aristotelian. Non-Aristotelian simply means not according to thought solidified by Aristotle's followers for nearly 2,000 years. Van Vogt (like Korzybski) postulated that to the degree your thinking and experiencing was non-Aristotelian the more likely you are to be sane and to the degree that your thinking followed Aristotelian precepts, the more likely you are to be insane. This did not clarify anything for me. All I knew was that I experienced Gilbert Gosseyn, Van Vogt's hero, as a person who seemed to abstract from his experiencing of reality rather than impose his abstractions on reality. This meant something to me because I was aware of my own growth when I stopped projecting my own expectations and evaluations on the world and attempted to experience it (as much as is possible) as it is.

My next step was to try to understand better Korzybski's ideas as he

*Unpublished paper, 1972.

writes them in his book *Science and Sanity.* Korzybski is the founder of the science of General Semantics which, in very simple terms, is the endeavor to understand the meaning of words (further clarification must be your own). His ideas are thus rooted in the nature of language and he has managed to apply them to large areas of human endeavor.

Korzybski has been particularly diligent in relating his ideas to man and his sanity. He proposes that language and thinking are part and parcel to one another (not a new idea). Each affects and, in turn, is affected by the other. Our language habits including how we talk — whether our language is specific or general, descriptive or judgmental — and our attitudes toward our own remarks — whether dogmatic or openminded, rigid or flexible — affect how we act and respond to our world and the people in it. Thus, Korzybski sees words as more than descriptions of the territory of human experience; they are evaluations. How we think is bound up in how we talk so that if our spoken evaluations are hasty and ill-considered our unspoken ones are likely to be even more so. For example, a man says "I don't like fish," although there are thousands of different types of fish and dozens of different ways to prepare them. Because he "doesn't like fish" he avoids clams, oysters and lobster which are not even related to fish. All prejudices work in this same way. Hence, unexamined key words in our thought processes such as "fish" or "free enterprise" or "military mind" or "the Jews" can create the illusion of meaning where no clear-cut meaning exists and come to hinder or misdirect our thoughts.

Following this line of reasoning, Korzybski feels that such misuse of language and words pervades our society and is the source of its insanity. The problem, although partly due to the inadequacy of language itself, also is derived from the way most of us reason, make inferences and build abstractions. Language tends to follow the lines of these processes and vice versa. Korzybski never gets around to resolving which happens first, hinting that both may be related to neural structure. The majority of us tend to reason along the lines of Aristotelian science and its associated metaphysical and philosophical assumptions. Although much of the content of Aristotle's science has long been disproved, the underlying assumptions have remained to influence most of the science, philosophy, and even religion which man has devised in the past two thousand years. It has only been with the advent of non-Euclidian geometry and Einstein's Theory of Relativity that Aristotle's basic assumptions have been challenged. Many of us still labor with Aristotelian thought coloring our attitudes, beliefs, and feelings in our everyday transactions.

The trouble with Aristotle, according to Korzybski, consisted of the three basic assumptions upon which he built his view of the world. Because the assumptions were wrong any "map of the territory" (knowledge of reality) that is abstracted based upon their being true will be a distorted and ineffective map of that territory. Since many of our language and consequently our thought processes are patterned on these assumptions our abstractions from reality are likely to be distorted.

Very briefly, Aristotle postulated three laws as the basis for defining knowledge: the law of identity, the law of the excluded middle, and the law of non-contradiction. All were based on Aristotle's belief of permanence in the world. Thus he reasoned that a thing is one thing only and permanently remains that thing. He used simple propositional statements to define and identify objects: "grass is green," "water is wet," etc. He further assumed in his second law that anything is "A" or "non-A"; it cannot be both. A leaf is not a tree, for they exclude each other. In his third law, Aristotle assumed that "A" cannot be a part of "B" and still be "A." The application of this states that the leaf cannot be both itself and the tree at the same time.

As a consequence of these laws our language contains a number of semantic traps which, if we allow them, distort our view of the world. One trap lies in the assumption that there is a "permanence" to reality, an assumption that is denied by all the modern sciences. One fact we can be sure of is that reality is changing and always in the process of change. What we perceive as "permanence" is only a statistical summation of the world in process that is imposed on us by the limitations of our sensory and neural system. The trap is that because we assume permanence, the word becomes the thing and the "map becomes the territory." We then begin to behave as if we identified words with things. We would all agree the word "Negro" is not the same thing as Bob Adams, to whom that label is applied. Yet many of us would judge Bob Adams as though he were that label. When we do that, we put Bob Adams in a category, we classify him and then respond and behave towards him as though he were identical to every other person in that classification. A moment's reflection should reveal the fallacy in this. Bob Adams is not identical to every other person in the category of Negro but exhibits at every perceptual level (if one cares to make full use of one's senses) as many differences as he does similarities to the other persons subsumed under the label "Negro." In other words, Bob Adams is one of a kind in the universe. To respond to Bob Adams in any other way is not only doing Bob Adams injustice, but it is an injustice to the person responding in that way. Such a person is operating with an inadequate map of the territory and has decreased the flexibility with which he can respond to the world.

An accurate map can only be built with the recognition that Negro 1 is not Negro 2 is not Negro 3, ad infinitum, and then letting our experience and senses tell us how they are not. To go one step further, it must also be recognized that the Bob Adams of the example is not the same Bob Adams as he might have been yesterday. He has changed with the experiences he has had since then, and, if we are to have an accurate map of him we must reorganize our map to include our experience of those changes in him.

There is a second trap in Aristotle's second assumption, the law of the excluded middle. If we assume "anything is either A or non-A," then we look at the world in terms of opposites: black vs. white; evil vs. good; etc. We rule out the possibility of a continuum of experience and in the process deny everything that modern science can tell us about the universe as it is now known. To illustrate this idea, psychologists for many years got caught in the trap of seeing people as either introverts or extroverts because they accepted the assumption of an "either-or" world. It was not until someone extended themselves to admit to the evidence available; that some people could exhibit characteristics of both; that a middle group of ambiverts was recognized to exist. In the same way, we often label ourselves in one or several situations as "bad" or "stupid" or "incompetent" and then come to think of ourselves in those terms. Then, because we have come to think in terms of opposites, we cannot see ourselves as "good" or "smart" or "competent" or anything in between the polarities in situations where it is appropriate to experience ourselves as such. Again we have made false assumptions and drawn inferences from these which result in a false map of the territory which, in turn, limits our ability to respond flexibly to the world.

A third trap is represented by Aristotle's third law, that of noncontradiction. From this law comes our predilection to break things into parts or elements when we try to identify or define them. The fallacy in this can easily be seen from the earlier example of this law, that the leaf cannot be both itself and the tree at the same time. A tree, however, is not a tree without leaves because it would perish without them. Thus, modern science recognizes the importance of conceptualizing the world in terms of dynamic wholes. Not doing this lays us open to serious distortions in perceptions of reality. In psychotherapy, therapists often make the mistake of seeing the therapeutic situation as separate and isolated from the rest of the client's world. It is, to them, a separate and identifiable part of that world. They then become frustrated when their carefully planned efforts in the situation do not seem to effect change in a client. What they fail to see is that the therapy hour is only one factor that interacts with, influences, and in turn is influenced by other factors in the dynamic whole which is the client's life space. In the same way we may tend to see others in terms of parts rather than wholes. For example, we often form impressions of people on the basis of how we have seen them behave in only one or a few situations. Hence, an instructor whom we have contact with only in the limited confines of a classroom becomes for us that person we perceive in that one isolated situation. There he may be humorless, cold, and disciplined. We cannot recognize in him the possibilities of being the witty, warm, and perhaps irreverent person he may well be with his family and close friends. By not being able to make such a recognition we are not open to experiencing him as a whole person, unique and interesting in every way. Our map of the territory has again limited our ability to experience reality.

The insanity in us is rooted in our use of words and how we use them to make inferences and abstractions about reality. We begin from early childhood to use words (perhaps a better term is misuse) to classify and categorize all the world and all our own experience. In this process of categorization we begin to think of the world as if it were our words, our labels, and our abstractions, and move further and further away from our experiencing of it. In time our abstractions which are inferences from other abstractions become independent of the world as it is. We succeed in cutting ourselves off from our experiences as they are moment-to-moment and live in the dark world of our abstractions. Our perceptual world becomes concerned with problems of expectation, prediction, comparison, etc. We respond to situations not as they are but as we think they ought to be (from the past) or should be (from our fantasies of the future) and thus continually lose the "presentness" of our reality. When we find ourselves in situations when our abstracted "reality" does not quite fit reality as it is, we get disturbed. Rather than rechecking our own rigid preconceptions and formulations, we simply rearrange reality by denying or distorting our experiencing of it. The end result is that we end up evaluating reality in terms of our abstractions rather than evaluating our abstractions by checking them with our experiencing of reality as it actually is.

Insanity, then, in Korzybski's terms is caused by assuming that our mental map *is* the territory and is accurate without checking reference points for validation. The extreme of this can be seen in psychotics who behave without any reference to the real world outside them. They are using their own internal maps that may have no relation at all to reality. Their insanity is different only by degree from that of the rest of us. Psychotics have completely shut out their experiencing of reality while most of us still manage to admit enough experience to allow our map to bear some semblance to reality. However, one need only look at the prejudice, bigotry, and jealousy with which we treat one another to recognize that very few of us manage to maintain maps of the territory that contain any large degree of accuracy.

A definition of sanity can be achieved by reversing the focus. If insanity is the result of a poor map of the territory and mistaking the fluid, dynamic, real world for the static, rigid world of labels and categories, then the problem of sanity becomes one of learning how to make more accurate maps of the territory. Thus, to move toward sanity we must reverse our map-making process of imposing our abstractions on reality to that of abstracting reality from actual experiencing. We must become fact-oriented (extensional) rather than word-oriented (intensional). We must learn to perceive that the world is dominated by factual events (continually checking our experiencing) rather than concepts. We must become more capable of differentiation with awareness of both the space-time anchorage of experience and different levels of abstraction. We must allow our awareness to be characterized by openness rather than defensiveness, letting stimuli be freely relayed through our nervous system without distortion.

Carl Rogers (1951) summarizes this openness by suggesting that rather than perceiving in predetermined categories ("Southerners are Democrats," "Winters are cold") the individual is aware of this existential moment as it is, thus being alive to many experiences which may fall outside the usual categories ("this Southerner is an Independent," "This winter is balmy"). Armed with this extensional orientation we have increased our ability to build more accurate maps because we continually validate them by checking the territory with our own experiencing. Moreover, our maps become dynamic because as features of the territory actually change we are able to reorganize our maps. Thus, our evaluations of reality are based on experience (or facts) rather than ideas, words, or concepts.

A good illustration of this extensional orientation just described can be seen in children. They have not yet learned all the labels and categories and thus they have not learned to become concerned with the problems of expectation and prediction. Children's worlds are primarily worlds of the immediate and they do not respond, to any large degree, in terms of expectations, either their own or others. As an example, several years ago I was involved in administering individual intelligence tests to small children for a course I was taking in the use of the Wechsler and Stanford Binet tests. When I asked children (mostly four- and five-year-olds) for a definition, the characteristic response would go something like this:

> "What is a truck?"
> "A truck is a truck."
> "But can you tell me in your own words what it is?"
> "A truck is a truck."
> "Yes, but tell me what a truck is."
> "I did."

Such responses bothered me, but like others, I assumed that these responses were an inability to conceptualize, to describe the object or to categorize it. As I look back on it now, those children in their failing attempts to pass the test were actually showing their wisdom. As adults we come to view trucks as something that is "a vehicle" or is "metal" rather than seeing the truck as made of metal or constituting one of a class of "vehicle." In raw experience, however, the truck is a truck. In recognizing this those children were responding to their own experience rather than adult expectations involving higher levels of abstraction, description, and categorization. They were responding in a simple,non-abstracted extensional way.

The fundamental allegation of this paper is that an individual or group counseling experience can facilitate changes in our perceptual processes very much like what is needed if we are to live saner lives. The changes I have noticed in myself and others as a result of participating in a group, for example, seem always to include a greater openness to experiencing the world as it is rather than how I conceptualize it. In me this is coupled with an attitude that can best be described as "believing it so does not make it so." I seem now always to start with a negative judgment about my abstractions which ends up as "I could be wrong; let's recheck the facts (my experiencing of a situation)." The rechecking usually involves all my experience, not just what I see and hear, but especially the sensory messages that I get from my body — what I am feeling. It is only when I have done this that I feel comfortable that my perceptions are reasonably accurate at that point in time. It is when my perceptions of the world fit my actual experiencing of it (what Rogers would call congruence) that I experience myself as sane.

Toward Being Sane: Some Common Futilities

Mowrer's notion that we often mistake thought-symbols in the form of words and language for reality describes a common and usually futile effort at living successfully by trying to understand. There are several other terms and concepts representing common futilities that are central in Gestalt theory and techniques. Among these are words, understanding (knowing) and being understood, seeking and giving approval. Some thoughts on these are presented here using the first person and masculine gender for the sake of convenience and ease of expression.

The Futility of Words

In addition to the abstraction-reality difficulties that accrue from language as described by Mowrer, there are the problems of time and intention. A fundamental problem with words, for example, is that, in whatever time is required to choose and say words, not to mention the time needed for conceptualization, the moment passes. The actual tense becomes the past and in it I tell about only what I remember. Further, this recollection is highly selective since none of us is blessed with total awareness. At any point in time my awareness is focused upon only those elements that seem to have significance for me. When I tell about it later (the only possible time), I am able to recall and describe only a fragment of all the things I experienced in that moment. Two kinds of distortion can occur. One comes from believing that the past and the present are synonymous; the other occurs by assuming that conscious awareness can include all important forms of experience. Both types of distortion happen frequently and contribute in important ways to feelings of emptiness, confusion and unhappiness.

A primary *motive* in using words is to explain — to justify myself toward helping you understand me. In doing this I believe that if you understand what it is like to be me then you will see how blameless or helpless or correct or justified I am in feeling (or not feeling) or acting (or not acting) as I do (or do not). In hoping you will find me faultless, I manifest (1) a request for your approval and (2) a belief that your approval would give me peace, confidence, authority or whatever else I think I need. These assumptions, of course, are invalid.

The Futility of Knowing

It was pointed out earlier that the human being's nature is to wonder. These wonderings often take the form of questions such as the following: Why do I act this way? What's wrong with me? What should I do? How can I get what I want? How can I keep from getting in trouble? These and similar questions seem to be the bane of human existence; we all wonder this way at times.

Underlying a question of this sort is the notion that there is an *answer*, a proper and satisfying solution. It is further assumed that the answer can be arrived at by introspection, analysis, and logic. In order for this assumption to stand, another even more basic belief must be held: the concept of absolutes referred to by Mowrer. No further discussion of this concept is necessary here, but Gestaltists point out that in the realm of feelings, emotions, values and attitudes — the stuff of which most behavior consists — there are few absolutes.

A common goal of counseling, therapy, and discovery activity is to enable clients to experiment with their own polarities and ranges of experience and expression. It seems manifestly true that each of us can discover the ways in which his own organism is most congruent with its environment in relation to subjective phenomena. Congruence is experienced emotionally, sensorially, and cognitively rather than merely being known or understood in the conventional sense. In the Gestalt frame of reference, therefore, the question becomes, "What do you think/feel/believe at this time?" The "right" answer — the one that most accurately describes the person's awareness at the time — may be different from one moment to the next.

The Futility of Being Approved of

Another typical motive for wanting to "know" something is in order to conform with some external (someone else's . . . whose?) criterion — expectation, social mode, standard, etc. — so that we get the approval we seek. This seeking is usually experienced as a need. Gestaltists observe that there are a few genuine needs in the ordinary course of life and encourage clients to recognize that they are actually speaking of "wants," however strong they may be. More will be said of this later in the discussion of techniques. By literally knowing the rules that we believe others demand we live by, we can know how to behave. All behavior thus becomes public performance, acting, and is intentionally chosen to avoid not-being-disapproved-of. Living and behaving are then essentially defensive and are engaged in for the purpose of surviving and avoiding existential death.

The trouble with this sort of existence is that it may have very little to do with the real and total person who is only perceiving rules with his mind, then acting out the perceived behavioral instructions. The individual becomes unreal, phony, empty, non-authentic. There is no allowance for experiencing *his own* awareness of things, pleasant or unpleasant. Pleasant feelings are experienced at most as breaking even — neither winning nor losing — by following the rules well so that disapproval is avoided. This kind of contentment is temporary and fragile. Even unpleasant feelings can be artificial and vapid since their origin is outside the person; they are occurring because of someone else's rules. It usually goes like this: "I am feeling bad because I didn't do what one or both of us thought I should do, and therefore I don't qualify for receiving your approval (that I have come to believe I need)." The bad feelings I have are not based upon my own, authentic awareness of the circumstances. They are happening because I have failed to act properly — the way I thought someone else wanted me to. Even my bad feelings, then, are someone else's. I feel empty somehow and unreal. And always in my sadness or depression or guilt there is a deep and hidden anger in me toward you for "putting" these feelings in me.

In these brief definitions of some of the futilities encountered in the processes of thinking and talking, there can be seen some origins of non-authenticity as a function of misdirected focus, lack of awareness, assignment of motives to others, and conflicting desires. The goal of Gestalt counseling and therapy is to assist the client in achieving a fuller integration of cognitive, affective, and sensory experience. The following section contains descriptions of methods used in the Gestalt approach to counseling toward attaining this goal.

Counseling Methods

Language Rules

There is a common philosophical theme among many in the humanistic movement that life is a process of learning, changing, and becoming. In order to live fully one must do these things. Gestaltists observe that such efforts are not only useless but actually work against the organism's innate systems. One who *is* needn't try to *be;* a dynamic organism needn't *try* to change. The most useful activities, therefore, are awareness of present experience, focusing, recognition, and "owning" of perceptions, choosing, and acting. The objective is simply to discover and become aware of how I am at this moment.

Several references have been made previously to the language-abstraction-reality dilemma. A useful method for assisting others to recognize reality rather than some abstraction of it is to encourage the use of accurate and specific language. These are often referred to as language rules. They are more accurately described as language guidelines to discovery.

Clients are encouraged to say "I think" rather than "I know." This reflects the reality that little in life is entirely certain. The speaker acknowledges that a given phenomenon may be perceived differently by others and that there is no single correct perception. The statement then becomes mine — this what I think/feel at this time and I take responsibility for it.

Example:

Client: I know I shouldn't feel this way.
Counselor: Try that sentence again using the word "think" instead of the word "know."
Client: I think I shouldn't feel this way. Yeah, that's right. I really don't know what I should feel but I think some other way would be better than this.

By the same token it is unusual to genuinely "need" anything. This term's use can be restricted to physiological matters so that any other motive or request can be seen and experienced in a more accurate, real perspective by using the word "want." It is not something my body or soul or happiness or any other fragment must have in order to exist; neither is it a function of external circumstances or persons. I "want" it, whether or not my motive is understood at this time.

Example:

Client: I need him to tell me that it's OK for me to have my own interests.
Counselor: What would it be like if you'd say "want" rather than "need"? Try it.
Client: OK. I want him to tell me that it's OK for me to have my own interests.
Counselor: Is this different in any way?

Client:	Hmmm . . . yes, there is . . . I don't actually need his approval. It's just that I'd like him to acknowledge that I'm a person, too, and that my life is more than just doing the things he wants me to.

The words "they" and "it" are common terms that typically serve to mask the speaker's truth and keep him or her from recognizing that some person(s) is often the actual topic of his conversation. Upon hearing either of these words, the counselor urges the client to identify who is being discussed.

Example:

Client:	The trouble is that they don't listen.
Counselor:	Who is the "they" you refer to?
Client:	What? . . . uh, I'm not sure . . . oh, yeah. It's the people I work with, but mostly it's my boss. He never really hears me.

Example:

Client:	It's too hard. I can't do it.
Counselor:	What is the "it"?
Client:	Telling my parents that I want to get an apartment. I'd have to tell them I'm unhappy here and they'd be hurt.
Counselor:	So the "it" actually refers to saying the truth to your parents about what you want? Is this what you can't do?
Client:	I'm not sure . . . well, maybe, but it will be hard to do.

In this same vein, clients are asked to replace "I can't" statements with "I don't want" statements. The purpose is to aid the client in regaining his or her integrity and ability to choose (decide). The term "can't" suggests that the person is unable to act for reasons over which he or she has no control and this is rarely the case. The speaker assigns, intentionally or inadvertently, some measure of personal authority to some abstraction or circumstance.

Example:

Client:	I just can't seem to concentrate.
Counselor:	Try that sentence again and this time say I "don't want to" rather than "I can't."
Client:	I just don't want to concentrate. That's not true, I do.
Counselor:	Stay with the sentence for a moment. Try it again and see what happens. Could it possibly be true for some reason?

Client: (Repeats, pauses) You know, I don't like that course at all. I'd rather do anything but study for it.

Gestaltists recognize that more than one motive, feeling, or idea can exist at a time. The fact that one or more may be in conflict does not mean that only one can be true. The client is encouraged to use "and" rather than "but." In this way he or she can discover all the things that are true rather than pretending that some are not. The final step then becomes one of facing the entire picture of reality and making a choice with maximum awareness of the alternatives.

Example:

Client: Sometimes I feel like yelling at the kids, but I don't hate them.

Counselor: Could you say that again, only this time use "and" in place of "but?"

Client: (Repeats as suggested) That sounds crazy, but . . . oops! . . AND it's true! I love them and there are times when I get very mad at them. Yes, both are true.

Gestalt-oriented counselors are notorious for their attention to splits in awareness, the conceptual division of the total self into categories of thought, feeling, attitude, ability and so on. Such common phrases as, "I see myself as . . . ," and "I think I . . . ," appear to be innocuous; further, they are much in vogue. However, they are insidiously fragmenting, since the speaker exists in the sentence as both subject and object, and there is some likelihood that he or she may actually experience being both, and consequently neither. There are two alternative responses to statements containing these phrases. More will be said later about asking the client to "be" both persons. The language-focus technique consists of directing the client to eliminate the duality by using simpler, more direct language that moves the client closer to reality.

Examples:

Original statement: I think I can.
Preferred: I can.
Original statement: I see myself as being flexible.
Preferred: I'm flexible.
Original statement: I'm feeling some anger.
Preferred: I'm angry at him.

The matter of tense is crucial in Gestalt counseling. The words clients use indicate occasions when present awareness either is getting lost or is being avoided, whether or not the flight is consciously intended. Perls described thought related to the future as rehearsal and thought related to the past as remembering. In either case, there is a loss of contact with present awareness that can be regained by encouraging the use of the present tense. This method does not rule out attention to prior events or those the client may anticipate; it merely brings them into a present, here-and-now focus that is real. Reference to the future follows words such as "if," "when," and "then." Some element from the past is usually still present when clients use words and phrases such as "It used to be . . . ," "I remember . . . ," "When . . . ," and ". . . before." One technique consists of having the client create the remembered or anticipated scene here-and-now, taking the parts of all persons and significant elements in turn using the present tense. The language guideline involves merely asking the client to stay in the present by using the present tense.

Example:

Client:	I was a little nervous before coming here.
Counselor:	What are you feeling now?

Example:

Client:	If that happens then I'll faint.
Counselor:	Can you describe your feelings about it at this moment?

Breathing and Relaxation

An excellent means of enabling clients to experience the discovery and awareness that are central in the Gestalt approach to counseling is focusing upon breathing and physical sensations. These activities can serve to teach relaxation methods the client can use at will and, perhaps more importantly, demonstrate the concept of "allowing" one's awareness to focus so that reality can emerge. Several descriptions of relaxation techniques are available in published form and can also be improvised as can a variety of breathing activities. Examples of each are provided for illustration:

Counselor:	Make yourself as comfortable as possible in the chair. Try to sit so that the chair is supporting every part of your body. Close your eyes. Become aware now of your breathing, as fully aware as you can be, and notice everything you think and feel. (Pause) Now allow yourself to expand your breathing, both inhaling and exhaling quite deeply and fully with your mouth and throat

open and unrestricted. Do this a few times and be aware of what it's like. (Pause) Now allow your breathing to normalize, to be full, easy and regular without straining. Continue this for a while.

At this point the client can be invited to tell about the experience and what it was like. He or she can then be asked to describe what's happening at this moment, so that the here-and-now focus is maintained. Most people discover that it's very difficult to maintain muscular and emotional tension after the free, life-sustaining, constantly-available process of full and easy breathing is achieved. We must choose to be tight! And we can choose to be more fully breathing and alive.

This procedure, beginning with present awareness, followed by relaxation instructions, followed by continuing directed focus, can be used with either overall body awareness or with emphasis upon such particular sensations as touch, muscle tone, posture position, etc. A segment of a relaxation activity follows:

Counselor: Become as comfortable as you can in the chair, allowing it to support you fully. Close your eyes now and let your awareness go to those parts of your body where you experience any pressure or tightness. Take your time and tell about these sensations as fully as possible. (Pause, letting the client report until it appears that he or she is no longer involved in the telling.) Now take a few minutes and allow your body to relax even more fully. Direct your attention to your toes. Notice what you are experiencing in that part of you, relax there and move on to your feet. (This is repeated until all parts of the body have received attention.) What occurred to you during this time? Describe what you feel physically at this moment.

Clients often discover significant messages while doing these activities. Occasionally a deeply meaningful response will occur that warrants additional attention and exploration. When this happens the relaxation activity can either be terminated or interrupted for as long as necessary while the client shifts attention to some other theme.

The arts of timing and focusing cannot be adequately described here. It must suffice to say that cues come from one's comprehensive awareness of the client. With practice and feedback a counselor can become increasingly confident and effective in relation to these vital competencies. A suggested sequence of training experiences will be described in a later section.

Locating Feelings

There are so many things that could be said about emotions that nothing can be said. Except that they exist. Clients are frequently able to say what they feel but cannot be articulate in describing the sensation nor can they understand having them, where they come from, or what purpose they may serve. A technique for aiding a client to become more in touch with a given feeling is to ask, "Where in your body are you aware of the feeling?" Some feel sadness in their chests, others in the abdomen. A given client can feel certain kinds of sadness in one place and other kinds in some different part of the body. It can also happen that the same sort of sadness will be felt in different parts of the body on different occasions. Patterns are difficult to discern and might serve no useful purpose in any case. The relationship between emotional and physical functioning is known to exist, however, and this knowledge can be used in facilitating a client's contact and discovery processes. When a feeling has been located in the body, for example, the client can then be asked to describe what that part of him/her is like at this moment. What does that feeling inside you look like — size, color, texture, etc.? Such a conversation might seem to make no sense at all if it weren't for the fact that responses having meaning for clients often emerge.

Stop Trying to Be Sane

Encouraging someone to be however he/she is may be good advice, but is a message that makes no sense at all to some. A person who has been conditioned to be logical, thoughtful, consistent, conforming, and self-reliant may have become so accustomed to using external, past, and future referents that subjective reality is only a concept. Progress may be hastened by speaking more directly to the person's old habits as follows:

Counselor: During the time we are together please dismiss any urge you may have to think, try, be sane, understand or act intelligently. Allow your thoughts and feelings to happen without monitoring or screening or deciding whether they should. As you allow your thoughts and feelings to come out as they will after you've stopped managing them we can find out more of what's real and important for you. Act the way you feel, even if that's angry, silly, sad, impolite, confused, or bored.

Opinions vary among Gestaltists concerning whether the counselor should make this explicit statement or whether it is more useful for the client to discover that this condition is a part of the relationship. We favor making the ground-rules common knowledge. In either case there is a tendency for most people to get better at behaving spontaneously with practice and there is typically a concomitant gain in self-awareness.

Polarities

By the time most of us have reached maturity we have developed certain styles of expressing each of the basic emotions, and it then seems as though these forms of behavior are made of steel; they are permanent and unchangeable. The following statements are characteristic: "I can't show affection openly"; "When I'm mad I yell and scream no matter who's around"; "If I disagree with someone I'll either reason with them all day or forget it — I'd never tell anyone off."

The fact is that emotions are more accurately described as multi-dimensional or non-dimensional rather than being static in either nature or intensity. Clients can be reminded that emotions are at least variable in intensity; one can be either miffed or furious, content or ecstatic. In this spirit a client can be encouraged to experiment a bit with various emotions:

Counselor: Show me how you act when your feelings have been hurt.

Client: (Does so quietly, with head and shoulders slumped)

Counselor: Good. Do it again and this time let the hurt soak in deeply, then get in touch with the feelings for a moment or two, then let it all out.

Client: (Slumps completely into the chair, moaning loudly, hands rubbing and pressing head, rumpling hair.)

Counselor: OK. Do it one more time, and this time show what you'd act like if the other person didn't matter much to you or that the incident was just a misunderstanding.

Client: (Grimaces, catches breath slightly, then speaks) Damn, it hurts to hear that.

Counselor: You've responded three different ways to the same hurtful situation. Does one way fit you better than the others?

Some people who find this procedure difficult to enact may be able to employ a mask or an "alias personality" more successfully. This can be done by acting out happiness, say, first as Scrooge and then as Zorba. The client selects one or more characters from literature, history, TV, the movies, etc., who would express a given emotion in dramatically different ways, then demonstrates how these personalities would react. By experimenting in this way with range, intensity, and style, a more appropriate and satisfying style of response can be discovered.

Exaggerating Physical Movements

As clients talk about their concerns in counseling sessions they often become animated. This may involve gestures with the hands, arms, legs, torso, and face. At the opposite extreme, some may become immobile as they talk. In either case, the client may be saying something with his or her body, a message that neither the client nor the counselor understands.

As awareness of these potential "body messages" develops the counselor may wish to invite the client to "discover" what he or she is doing. These movements must often be exaggerated in order for the client to experience their impact. For example, the client may be making a fist and lightly hitting the arm of the chair while making a point, verbally. The dialogue might continue in this way:

Counselor: Can you exaggerate that movement, hitting the chair?

Client: What do you mean?

Counselor: Your hand is in a fist and you are hitting the arm of the chair. Can you exaggerate that movement and hit the chair with more force?

Client: (Begins hitting the chair harder until he is pounding it.)

Counselor: What are you pounding? Who are you pounding?

Client: All those damned people who won't listen to me.

It is important that the meaning of any gesture or postural expression be discovered by the client. When he or she cannot give meaning to a gesture, it may indicate either that the counselor's timing was off or that the client continues to block awareness.

Should this happen, no more issue should be made of the event so that the client can proceed toward more profitable exploration.

The Empty Chair

The empty chair is a dialoguing exercise that is used to help the client explore and develop awareness when splits in awareness occur. The exercise is best suited to those splits that involve another individual or individuals (multiple splits). The only requirements are (a) an empty chair, and (b) the client's imagination. The counselor asks the client to talk to the person who he or she imagines to be occupying the empty chair. Then the client moves to the empty chair, occupies it him/herself, but in the role of the other person, and responds to him/herself (the client). This exercise can reveal to the client his or her expectations of the other person, including what the client expects the other person to give, and his or her response or reaction to that. The activity serves to clarify relationships and focuses the client's awareness on his or her part of those relationships. An example of a husband and wife relationship may illustrate this technique (the wife is the client).

Client:	(Talking to husband in empy chair) You never tell me what you are feeling, so how can I help you with your feelings?
Counselor:	Now change chairs and be your husband responding.
Client:	(As husband) I do tell you about my feelings. I tell you that I have had a hard day or that the boss was a bastard. You never wanted to hear my feelings.
Counselor:	Now change chairs again and be yourself responding.

There are two distinct advantages to be derived from this technique: (a) the client's defenses that characterize the relationship tend to diminish as she enacts the dialogue, thus permitting her to see elements of the relationship that she could not let herself see if her husband were actually present, and (b) the client is unable to maintain the insanity (distortion) that is part of the relationship, the insanity that is fed by the missing partner.

Being the Elements

Splits to awareness develop as the individual loses contact with the elements of his or her environment. A technique that helps renew that contact, and as a result, helps the client to re-focus attention is the projected dialogue which we shall refer to as "being the elements." The elements may be people (family members, group of friends, co-workers); they may be parts of a fantasy (objects, events, relationships between objects and events such as the passing of time); or they may be parts of a dream.

By "being" the elements, the client is asked to assume the role of the various elements and to enter into a dialogue with other elements and with the client. Where a male client may be experiencing difficulties in his family relationships, he may be asked to be his wife speaking to him, to be each of his children speaking to one another and to him, and to be himself responding to each of them. In effect, a theatrical setting is produced by the counselor who also acts as director. The client is the one and only actor and plays out the roles of each character in the event. This technique is an obvious extension of the empty chair and realizes the same advantages. It allows the client to view interactions of elements with less guardedness and defensiveness. It also allows him to step out of his insanity and perceive the interactions with better understanding.

Dreamwork

An extension of being the elements is dreamwork. Clients may occasionally refer to some dream they have had with the feeling that it has some unclear relevance to their problems. The mere mention of the dream at a time when problems are being discussed is considered evidence to this relevance. The dream may be a recurring one or it may have occurred only once. It may include significant others, significant settings, or strangers and strange settings. Regardless of its content, the counselor's objective in working with dreams is to use the dream medium to help the client identify conflict points, splits in awareness, or significant individuals who are related to the client's problems. All elements of the dream are projections of the client's awareness and their significance is available for discovery.

Again, it is not the counselor's role (it is not even within his or her potential) to make these identifications. Rather, it is the client who must be assisted in identifying and discovering the significance of the people, events, or objects that are part of the dream. This is achieved by asking the client to role-play or take the part of each element that is identified in the dream. This is done in the present tense so that the client describes *being* that element *now*.

For example, a college student (we shall call her Linda) reported that she had had the following dream:

Linda: I was picked up by this very expensive limousine. When I got in, I was struck by the plushness of the

> seats, the fine woodwork on the dashboard, the extreme comfort. It was like all my needs were being taken care of. As we were driving I turned and noticed the driver for the first time. He was an Oriental and was dressed in this chauffeur's uniform. He was unusually concerned for my welfare and my needs. I really felt taken care of by him too. We drove to this large, impressive house. It sat on a knoll and it had huge pillars in front, like a Southern mansion. We got out of the car and went into the mansion which turned out to be a restaurant. I was relieved to discover this. Discovering it was a restaurant eased my concerns because I knew how to behave in a restaurant. After we were seated (the Oriental chauffeur and me) the waiter came and offered us menus to study. It was then I realized I was very hungry. We waited and waited for the waiter to return and take our orders but no one came. As I started to look around for our waiter, I noticed that all the other customers in the restaurant were Orientals and this surprised me. Finally I spotted our waiter, and I got up from the table and went to him and asked him to come take our order. He said he would be there momentarily. Again we waited for what seemed like a long time. Finally, I got up again and went to the waiter and asked him to please serve us. He apologized for the delay and asked us to move to another table where we would be served immediately. We were led out of the main dining room into another empty room that was all white and had one wall of glass windows. I sat down and then realized that there was only one chair at the table. I looked up to see the waiter and my chauffeur both smiling at me. Then I looked and saw for the first time that the windows had bars on them. I was trapped. For the first time, I realized that I was in a mental institution and I was the patient.

This dream reflects several significant people, objects, and events that the client can be asked to role-play. She could be asked to be the limousine, the chauffeur, the large mansion, the restaurant, the waiter, the Oriental clientele, the white secondary dining room, the table with only one chair, the windowed wall, the bars, the smiling waiter and chauffeur. To try to role-play all of these options would require quite a bit of time. So the counselor might select from this list a smaller number of enactments. In that case, it is best to enact each role-play in the sequence in which it occurred in the dream.

The role-play is a dialogue that the client carries on with herself. As a result, it demands that the client use her imagination, often "supplying" information or details that were not in the original dream. This may be difficult for some clients to do, and it may be necessary to illustrate what you would have the client do in order that she understand. For example, Linda was first asked to "be" the limousine.

Linda: What do you mean?
Counselor: Be the limousine. If you were the limousine and could talk, what would you be saying to Linda.
Linda: I still don't think I understand.
Counselor: All right. I'll give you some help. Let's pretend that I am the limousine and this is what I might be saying, "Hi, little one. Get in and let me show you how good I am."
Linda: OK. I think I know what you mean.
Counselor: Good. Now, you be the limousine. What would you be saying to Linda?
Linda: Hello, Linda! Get in and let me show you how good I can be for you. I want to wrap you in comfort and make you feel really good.
Linda: Thank you. I would like for you to do those things to me. I want to feel safe, secure, and comfortable.

This first segment may be abbreviated (as it was with Linda). Getting into the "spirit" of the exercise takes time and the counselor should not push the client to produce more dialogue than she feels is there.

As the client dialogues different parts of the dream, the counselor asks the client to identify any potential relevance of the enactment to her life. For example:

Counselor: Linda, is there any significance in the dialogue between you and the limousine?
Linda: No, except that I like to be taken care of, and I think a lot of people would like to have that. That doesn't seem too unusual.
Counselor: OK. Let's go on to the next part of the dream, the driver that you suddenly notice. Can you describe the driver again?

Linda:	Yes. He is a large, kindly looking man. He is Oriental. He doesn't smile or anything. But I can tell that he doesn't mean me any harm.
Counselor:	Will you be the chauffeur now, talking to Linda?
Linda:	Yes. Hello, Linda. I am glad you joined me. I have been worried about you. I want to be sure no harm comes to you. I want to help you decide where to go so you will make the right decision. I want to make these decisions for you because you can't make them for yourself.
Counselor:	Now be Linda and respond to the chauffeur.
Linda:	Alright, I will do what you say. I know you can make better decisions than I can. I will do what you think is best.
Counselor:	Linda, does the chauffeur remind you of anyone you know?
Linda:	Yes, my father.
Counselor:	Is he your father?
Linda:	Yes, he is.
Counselor:	You said he was Oriental.
Linda:	Yes. You can never tell what an Oriental is thinking, and that is the way it is with Dad. He never let me know where he was or what he was feeling.

Linda began to find meaning as she progressed through other elements of the dream with increasing investment. She was asked to be the large mansion talking to Linda, and the dialogue led her to identify the mansion as the imposing social system that she had been taught to respect and obey. Linda talked about her mixed emotions regarding the social system. She could feel lost in it and that brought on anger and resentment that was bigger than she.

Her discovery that the mansion was really a restaurant after she had entered it was also relevant to her. She compared the relief that she had experienced upon discovering the restaurant to the relief she also felt when she realized that the social system was something she was very familiar with and knew how to play. The waiter who appeared so solicitous yet did not serve her was a further extension of her frustration at being unimportant within the system.

As Linda took on the role of the other customers in the restaurant, it became apparent to her that they were society sitting in judgment of her. She identified this through the cue that they were faceless, thus she could not read their emotions. She drew the conclusion that they must be reacting to her, and the hiding of their emotions had to mean that judgment was harsh.

It was when Linda began to enact and interpret the final portions of her dream that the gestalt began to emerge. Finding herself alone in the second dining room — the total whiteness (the absence of stimuli), the discovery of the windowed wall that was covered with bars — led her to an intense emotional experience. She cried softly. The counselor asked her to talk about her tears. Where were they coming from? Who was she crying for?

Linda saw the final portions of the dream tying into an old fear. She confided that since she had been in high school, she had feared that she would "go crazy" someday and have to be committed to a mental institution. She said that while she was in high school, her father had had a nervous breakdown and had been in a mental hospital for several months. The mother had kept the details from the children, and they had had to create the details in their imaginations. Linda said she related strongly to her father and feared the same would happen to her. Feeling her weakness and vulnerability, identifying the chauffeur as her father who wanted to take care of her but on his own terms, feeling the pressure of "society," all of this Linda identified as the constant underlying heaviness that she carried around. She could also see that there were moments of strength, points at which she could exercise control. This came through her sense of the "roles" of society that she understood, and it was apparent to her in her ability to deal with the reluctant waiter.

Dreamwork is not a panacea in Gestalt therapy. It does not always give the client instant relief. It can offer material that the client can work with and thus generate awareness of underlying tensions. It allows the client to focus.

There are several guidelines to follow while working with dreams:

1. Have the client describe the dream from beginning to end without interruption as a beginning step.
2. Describe the procedure for role-playing the dream (dialoguing).
3. If the client appears uncertain about the process, give an example.
4. Be the "director" of the role-play. Ask the client to be each of the several parts of the dream.
5. Proceed with different parts of the dream in the order of their occurrence in the dream.

6. Do not allow yourself to make interpretations of the elements of the dream. Only the client can do that. Ask the client if he or she can find any relationships. If he/she cannot, proceed to the next part of the dream.

Reversal

This technique is similar to both the empty chair and the polarities methods but refers to specific behaviors a client may have expressed an inability to engage in. The instruction consists of nothing more than telling clients to do what they say they can't or won't do:

Example:

Client: I can't stop procrastinating, and I don't know why I do it.

Counselor: Show me right now all the things you do to avoid working and as you do this explain how doing these things is better than working.

Client: (Gets up, scurries about the room telling of fantasied nonproductive activities, how they are pleasant and work is stifling)

Example:

Client: I just can't bring myself to hug someone I like.

Counselor: If you like me, do what you'd like to do if you were able.

Client: (Gets up, puts arms lightly around the counselor's neck, then pulls him up firmly and hugs tightly around the chest) So this is what it's like. I love it. It's funny, but I'm giving and taking both. I've been afraid it was all taking and I never think I've earned any good feelings.

In these examples the clients learned that their problem had more to do with motivation or attitude than with lack of ability. In both cases a step toward discovering a more basic reality was taken.

Feeding Sentences

In the client-centered approach to counseling, a basic technique is reflection of feeling which serves to mirror client feeling and thought. There is a counterpart in the Gestalt approach that is referred to as feeding sentences. As the counselor either hears or senses themes, moods, unspoken messages, or metaphors, the client is asked to "try these on for size," to discover whether they are true. The client is asked first to say the sentence the counselor offers or to complete a partial sentence. Having spoken the words, the client then reports whether the statement was experienced as true. If in saying the sentence the client discovers that it is only partly accurate, it can be revised until the client finds the words that accurately reflect what is being experienced. This technique illustrates using rather than being used by language.

Example:

The client has spoken for some time about the good relationships among his family members, how well his parents treat him, and how much he loves them all. He speaks in a monotone, his head bowed down.

Counselor: May I feed you a sentence? (Client agrees) "I should be happy and I'm not." Say this back to me.

Client: I should be happy and I'm not. (Pause)

Counselor: Does it seem true as you say it?

Client: As a matter of fact, it does. But how can that be? (Pause) There's just not enough room there. I know exactly how everything is and will continue to be and so does everyone else. At school I'm fine but when I get home it's like I play the same old role day after day.

Example:

A client discusses several ways in which she feels defeated and frustrated in interpersonal relationships. A negative, hopeless, passive theme emerges.

Counselor: Let's try something here. Finish the following sentence a few times, giving a different response each time: "I defeat myself when I . . ."

Client: I defeat myself when I . . . act defeated.
I defeat myself when I . . . blame others for hurting my feelings.
I defeat myself when I . . . don't think more about ways of succeeding and getting what I want.

Diagnosis is antithetical to Gestalt therapy. Feeding sentences is a way of validating a recurring impression that seems to be emanating from the client but may only be a useless (for the client) clinical observation. If some degree of real meaning is present the client can use the mirroring and language-experiencing in finding a fuller awareness.

Logical Extension

Sometimes we do not let ourselves know what we have been thinking. An illustration is rehearsal, fantasies about an event that is anticipated to be unpleasant. In the usual case the client speaks of the event indirectly, as though a vision of it is only faintly visible by looking backward over the shoulder. If an attitude of approach-avoidance, look-but-not-see is apparent a gradual extension of logical consequence may enable the client to turn around and move closer:

Example:

The client has talked about some unsatisfactory aspects of her relationship with her fiancee.

Client:	His dependence on me made me feel important at first but it's becoming a drag now.
Counselor:	And if you told him so he'd . . . ?
Client:	. . . hang on even tighter . . .
Counselor:	. . . and that would be bad because . . . ?
Client:	. . . then I'd get mad . . . maybe run . . .
Counselor:	. . . and . . . ?
Client:	. . . I don't want that. I want him to love me and be with me but not need me and lean on me.
Counselor:	So if you told him this he'd come apart?
Client:	No, I don't think he would. He might pout a little, but he really isn't weak. He'd say, "Let's work it out."
Counselor:	What would that be like?

Each counselor response enables the client to tell more about something that hasn't happened and may seem never to have been considered. And yet the scene unfolds and the client faces the fears with present awareness.

Leaving Unfinished

A goal of Gestalt counseling and therapy is to identify and complete what Perls called unfinished business — events from the past or thoughts of the future that have been experienced but not integrated into consciousness. Left-over guilt, unexpressed affection and hurt continue to affect the person, maintaining influence over behavior in ways that are neither perceived nor comprehended. The human organism seeks closure, completed gestalts, growth, and progress. These cannot always be attained rapidly enough, no matter how favorable the circumstances in terms of client motivation and counselor competency. People, events, thoughts and feelings come and go in an unending stream so that the notion of having no unfinished business is non-real.

It may be appropriate to offer this observation to the client. If there is agreement some relief may follow from recognizing what is and is not realistically possible. On the other hand, a continued persistence to finish everything at once may identify a place to begin the therapeutic conversation. Clients can learn to live more satisfactorily with things as they are for now.

Example:

Client:	Nothing's happening . . . I'm flat.
Counselor:	How is it to be flat? Can you stay with it?
Client:	I don't want to. I feel like resting.
Counselor:	OK. So tell me what you've decided to do and end your statement with, " . . . for now."
Client:	There are still some feelings and ideas in me. I'm ready for them to come out but they don't. I'll invite them again later but I'm tired so I'm leaving it this way for now.
Counselor:	(Says nothing. A deal is a deal.)

Other phrases are, " . . . and this is my truth now," or, " . . . and this is how I am now." If some urgency or strong motivation to continue at a later time is present, the client can be assisted in deciding when this will be done and in owning the decision at this time. Other decisions can be made later, of course. Certain kinds of homework or behavioral strategies are frequently useful between sessions and these possibilities may be examined. A feeling that may not surface during counseling may arise while the client is involved in typical daily activities. A commitment to focus and tune in to certain events fully can enhance continuing discovery.

A Suggested Training Sequence

The current popularity and prominence of the Gestalt approach to counseling and therapy provide testimony to the potential therapeutic power of these methods. Gestalt therapy is far more than a collection of techniques; it is way of living, experiencing, perceiving and acting. The philosophy and practice of Gestalt are learned through a process of experience, study and practice that ordinarily spans a period of several months of intensive training or a few years of training on a part-time schedule. This may seem like a long time, but we point out that training for law, engineering, management, medicine and university teaching all require at least as much. Some paraprofessional counselor training programs are currently advertising sequences ranging from approximately 30 to as many as 90 hours. Even these quantities of streamlined training activities translate to weeks or perhaps months when done on a part-time basis and do not offer, in our judgment, either the challenge or the satisfactions of being competent in the use of Gestalt methods. Moreover, the majority who have completed a comprehensive Gestalt training program have done so while maintaining full-time professional careers in psychology, education, social work, religion, or management, to name a few.

Personal Awareness and Growth

We hold the firm conviction that persons who aspire to sponsor counseling or therapy of any kind for others should first examine, explore and discover how their own systems work. This is a completely necessary phase in preparing to use Gestalt methods. We stand in wonder with an attitude of some intolerance, frankly, at those counselors and therapists who have not participated in any kind of discovery experience and have neither acknowledged nor acted upon a wish for assistance in resolving a personal dilemma. In the heart of this attitude there is a hole — an absence of experienced realization that counseling can be an effective means of living with a fuller degree of control and perhaps joy.

Discovery and awareness can be achieved in such settings as sensitivity and encounter groups. Participation in a variety of orientations and methodological approaches can be both personally productive and educational. Personal counseling provides a different perspective, and the value of learning that one person can be a catalyst for another can be great. The counselor's only tool is his/her own self. The more one is aware and acceptant of oneself, the greater the likelihood that others will be served well.

Gestalt Experience

The Gestalt view of life is unique and distinct. The methodology cannot be comprehended apart from the philosophy, nor does either make complete sense until it has been experienced. Being a member of a Gestalt group or an individual client serves two purposes: (1) some additional discovery is almost bound to occur and this alone may be sufficient grounds, and (2) both experiences are opportunities to observe and learn from one already qualified.

Formal Study

There is a temptation to speak of ethics and professional responsibilities here. Much could be said in favor of reading, seminars, theory explication, and research that would not seem out of place.

In our constant human seeking for control and completion, however, there is a wish to see both the whole puzzle, to notice how the pieces fit together, and to enjoy having completed it. A real motive for being able to conceptualize and account for one's behavior as counselor or therapist already exists; no artifact need be created.

The number and quality of publications devoted to Gestalt theory and practice have increased markedly during the past five years or so. See, for example, Perls' *In and Out the Garbage Pail* (1969b) a vivid, sometimes startling self-description of the man, his life, and what he believed. His earlier publications are more esoteric but no less valuable (Perls, Hefferline and Goodman, 1951; and Perls, 1969a). Also highly recommended are *Gestalt Therapy Now* by Fagan and Shepherd (1970) and the more recent *Gestalt Therapy Integrated* by Polster and Polster (1973). An approach containing a blend of Transactional Analysis and Gestalt experiments is described in *Born to Win* by James and Jongeward (1971).

Practice and Feedback

At the Gestalt Institutes (in New York City, Cleveland, Atlanta, Chicago, San Francisco, and Los Angeles, for example) the student progresses as client and member through individual and group experience, then into a group co-leader (assistant) assignment, co-leading as a senior partner and offering individual therapy. During these stages there is continuing practice, observation and feedback from colleagues and trainers as learning occurs from experience and study. Throughout training attention is devoted to perceptual accuracy, timing, relevant creativity, spontaneity, awareness of others, awareness of self in relation to others, willingness to trust and risk, and such routine behaviors as style and delivery.

Becoming competent in the use of Gestalt methods and techniques is time-consuming and timeless, exhausting and exhilarating, frustrating and joyful.

BIBLIOGRAPHY

Bandura, A. *Principles of behavior modification.* New York: Holt, Rinehart and Winston, Inc., 1969.

Beck, C. E. *Philosophical foundations of guidance.* Englewood Cliffs, N.J.: Prentice-Hall, Inc., 1963.

Bergin, A. E., & Garfield, S. L. (Eds.) *Handbook of psychotherapy and behavior change: An empirical analysis.* New York: John Wiley and Sons, Inc., 1971.

Enright, J. B. An introduction to gestalt techniques. In Joen Fagan and Irma Lee Shepherd (Eds.), *Gestalt therapy now.* Palo Alto: Science and Behavior Books, Inc., 1970.

Fagan, J., & Shepherd, I. L. *Gestalt therapy now.* New York: Harper and Row, 1970.

Freud, S. *The problem of anxiety.* New York: W. W. Norton & Company, Inc., & the Psychoanalytic Quarterly Press, 1936.

Freud, S. *The interpretation of dreams.* Vol. 4. Standard Edition of the *Complete psychological works of Sigmund Freud,* London: The Hogarth Press & the Institute of Psycho-analysis, 1953.

Freud, S. *A general introduction to psychoanalysis.* New York: Washington Square Press, 1960.

Hall, C. S., & Lindzey, G. *Theories of personality.* New York: John Wiley and Sons, Inc., 1970.

Hilgard, E. R. *Theories of learning.* (2nd ed.) New York: Appleton-Century-Crofts, Inc., 1956.

James, M., & Jongeward, D. *Born to win.* Menlo Park, California: Addison Wesley Publishing Company, 1971.

Koffka, K. *Growth of the mind.* New York: Harcourt, Brace, & Co., 1924.

Köhler, W. *Mentality of apes.* London: Routledge & Kegan Paul Ltd., 1925.

Köhler, W. *Gestalt psychology.* New York: Liveright Publishing Corporation, 1947.

May, R. The origins and significance of the existential movement in psychology. In Rollo May (Ed.), *Existence.* New York: Basic Books, 1958.

Patterson, C. H. *Theories of counseling and psychotherapy.* New York: Harper and Row, 1966.

Perls, F. S. *Gestalt therapy verbatim.* Moab, Utah: Real People Press, 1969. (a)

Perls, F. S. In and out the garbage pail. Moab, Utah: Real People Press, 1969. (b)

Perls, F. S., Hefferline, R. F., & Goodman, P. *Gestalt therapy.* New York: Julian Press, 1951. (Republished: New York, Dell, 1965.)

Perls, F. S. Four Lectures. In Joen Fagan and Irma Lee Shepherd (Eds.), *Gestalt therapy now.* Palo Alto, Calif.: Science and Behavior Books, Inc., 1970.

Perls, L. One Gestalt therapist's approach. In Joen Fagan and Irma Lee Shepherd (Eds.), *Gestalt therapy now.* Palo Alto: Science and Behavior Books, Inc., 1970.

Polster, E., & Polster, M. *Gestalt therapy integrated.* New York: Brunner/Mazel Publishers, 1973.

Rogers, C. R. *Client-centered therapy.* Boston: Houghton Mifflin Company, 1951.

Shertzer, B., & Stone, S. C. *Fundamentals of counseling.* (2nd ed.) Boston: Houghton Mifflin Company, 1974.

Ullman, L. P., & Krasner, L. *A psychological approach to abnormal behavior.* Englewood Cliffs, N.J.: Prentice-Hall, Inc., 1969.

Van Vogt, A. W. *The world of Null-A.* New York: Berkley Publishing Corp., 1974.

Wallen, R. Gestalt therapy and Gestalt psychology. In Joen Fagan and Irma Lee Shepherd (Eds.), *Gestalt therapy now.* Palo Alto: Science and Behavior Books, Inc., 1970.

INDEX